Please Foto all of
gramma (page 3
to 149)

The
Grammar Review
Book

TO. Jane

NOV 18

About the Authors

David and Peggy Kehe have been teaching ESL for over 25 years. In the 1970s they spent two years teaching EFL as Peace Corps Volunteers in Niger, West Africa. After that, they taught for a year on Lesbos Island, Greece; for twelve years in colleges in Japan; and for a number of years in colleges in the United States. Currently, in Bellingham, Washington, David teaches TESL methodology and ESL, and Peggy is doing editing work. They both have MA degrees in Teaching ESL from The School for International Training in Brattleboro, Vermont. The cool greenery of rain forests serves as a backdrop for the lifestyle that they have established for themselves in the Pacific Northwest. Having no plants, pets, or kids allows them ample time to devote to writing and teaching, as well as to pursuing their passion for hiking in the Cascades.

Other Pro Lingua Books by David Kehe and Peggy Dustin Kehe

Conversation Strategies, 2nd edition. 29 Pair and group activities for developing communicative competence. 2005.

Discussion Strategies. Beyond everyday conversation. 2005.

Writing Strategies Book One: Intermediate. A student-centered approach. 2005.

Writing Strategies Book Two: Advanced. A student-centered approach. 2006.

Write after Input. Developing paragraphs and compositions from listenings and readings. 2008

The Grammar Review Book

Discovering and Correcting Errors

for anyone who has learned English by ear

David Kehe
and
Peggy Dustin Kehe

Pro Lingua Associates

Pro Lingua Associates, Publishers
P.O. Box 1348
Brattleboro, Vermont 05302 USA
Office: 802-257-7779
Orders: 800-366- 4775
Email: info@ProLinguaAssociates.com
WebStore www.ProLinguaAssociates.com
SAN: 216-0579

At Pro Lingua
our objective is to foster an approach
to learning and teaching that we call
interplay, the **inter**action of language
learners and teachers with their materials,
with the language and culture,
and with each other in active, creative
and productive **play.**

This book was designed by Susannah Clark. Cover design by Arthur A. Burrows. Printed
and bound by McNaughton & Gunn in Saline, Michigan.

Printed in the United States of America
First edition, second printing 2008. 2500 copies in print.

Preface

This textbook is designed to help learners improve their grammar. Many speakers of English have acquired an advanced level interlanguage that is adequate for most informal uses of the language. However, their grammar has errors and holes. The errors have often become "fossilized," and it takes a special effort to unlearn these problems. The holes show up when the learner is asked to perform in a context other than informal social interactional discourse; for example when a student is asked to write in a formal or academic style.

Often, the problems are barely noticeable because these learners have acquired English from an early age, and they may sound very much like native speakers. These speakers of English are sometimes referred to as ear-learners because they have constructed a grammar primarily from spoken input by listening to others. Many of these speakers are also known as Generation 1.5, the children of first generation immigrants. Typically, they have grown up in a home where English is not spoken, and they have picked up English "on their own." As a result, they lack some of the skills of a true second generation English speaker. Furthermore, they are likely to have developed their own set of rules for English structure — and their rules may often be wrong or inadequate. For many of these aural learners, their misconceptions become fossilized over time. As a result, they can find it difficult to overcome their errors, especially when they are taught with typical deductive grammar books, where a rule is given and the students are asked to apply it to a series of sentences.

The Grammar Review Book addresses the unique characteristics of this student population by guiding them inductively toward accurate understanding and use of grammatical structures. Although the exercises in the text were designed to appeal particularly to ear-learners, they can be very helpful for any English language speaker who is still struggling with the tricky areas of English grammar. The exercises incorporate the following four features:

1. **The exercises involve inductive rather than deductive thinking.** Each unit focuses on a specific grammatical structure, but the unit does not begin by introducing a rule. Instead, students start off by working through a series of examples and exercises. These are designed to give students the opportunity to intuit for themselves the rules that govern the structure that is the focus of the unit. When students have developed a rule by themselves, they are likely to apply it successfully as they continue to use the language.

2. **The exercises activate analytical skills.** Traditional grammar exercises often adhere to a pattern practice format, and many learners are able to successfully complete grammar exercises that follow a pattern. However, these students may remain unable to apply the rules that they have practiced in traditional exercises to other situations such as writing formal or academic English. To help students internalize a grammar rule, *The Grammar Review Book* goes an extra step by asking students to analyze and explain on their own the specific grammar rules that govern correct usage.

3. **There are multi-sensory exercises.** Since many English speakers have acquired much of the language by listening and speaking, this text includes oral/aural work. This is a format that is familiar to them, and one in which they are likely to excel.

4. **In the culminating exercise in each unit, students apply the grammatical focus of the unit to an original writing task.** Applying their grammatical knowledge to assignments in which they generate original work gives students a richer, more meaningful, and more practical learning experience.

Table of Contents

As this book is based on improving the learner's grammar, the basis for each unit, except for the introductory and review units, is to fix a recurring grammatical mistake. In this table of contents, examples of mistakes are listed after the title of the unit.

Acknowledgements

We would like to thank **Patti Braimes** for her suggestions and encouragement. As a result of her involvement, The Grammar Review Book went through several additional stages of drafts and revisions; based on her advice, new exercises were added, and others were redesigned. In fact, without the input and energy that Patti provided, The Grammar Review Book might still be a rough draft sitting in a file.

Also, a special thank you goes to **Kathy Cook**, whose contributions in the later stages of development were invaluable.

— DK and PDK

User's Guide

This book is a **student-centered text**. In other words, the teacher and the text organize the students' work in the classroom, but the students work on the book individually or in pairs or even small groups. Teacher-talk is reduced to a minimum, and this also allows the teacher the opportunity to monitor the students' work and assist individuals as the need arises. The following procedure has been effective:

1. The teacher briefly **introduces** the main point(s) of the unit. One way to do this easily and effectively is to point out the "The Problem" (the typical mistake) that is located under the title of each unit.

2. The students **work on the exercises** individually or in pairs or small groups up to the last two exercises in the unit. The directions are clearly worded and user-friendly so the students will be able to proceed through the exercises without additional support from the teacher.

3. After the students have completed the exercises, they **check them in groups**. If they did the exercise with a partner or group, they should find a new partner or group to have a different set of eyes check the answers. When there is disagreement, the teacher can become involved. It can be especially effective if the teacher helps the students resolve the problem and figure out the answer by asking leading questions rather than by simply telling them the "correct" answer.

4. The teacher reads the **next-to-last exercise** in the unit. This is, in effect, a short **listening comprehension** exercise in the form of a **dictation** which incorporates the grammar point of the unit. Notice that in Units 1-10, the students have part of the sentence and are listening for the "gaps." This is the least challenging kind of dictation. In Units 11-20, the students have single-word cues and must construct more of the

dictated sentence. In the final units, the students are required to capture and produce the entire sentence. The scripts for these exercises are found in the back of the book.

5. The students do the **last exercise** in the unit on their own, applying the grammar point to a short, original **writing** task. This can be done in class or as homework. It is the only exercise that the teacher would need to check.

The **Grammar Groups** Units, which serve the purpose of reviewing the previous units, are also designed to be done with a minimum of teacher input. In addition to reviewing the grammar, the students may also discover that they can learn a lot from each other, helping them become more effective in coooperative learning contexts and ultimately becoming more confident and independent as learners.

A brief **glossary** of grammatical terms is included in the back of the book for reference purposes.

For the students, there is a chart of **common irregular verbs** following the glossary.

An **answer key** is available on www.ProLinguaAssociates.com, as well as in printed form.

Unit 1: Nouns

Exercise 1:   Look at the words in boxes and answer the questions below.

1. The ⬛hat is on the table .
2. I gave the man some money .
3. Tom moved his computer to a new desk .

Question 1: What do all the boxed words have in common?

   a) They show action.

   b) People can see and touch them.

   c) They are types of emotions.

Question 2: What do we call the boxed words?

   a) nouns   b) verbs

Exercise 2:   Circle the nouns that people can see and touch.

1. The baby ate some rice.

2. My brother drove his car to the ocean.

3. The rain was good for the flowers.

Exercise 3:   Look at the words in boxes and answer the question below.

1. Love is a wonderful thing.
2. Fear of snakes is quite common.
3. Anger causes problems for some people.

Question: What can we say about these boxed words?

   a) They are nouns that we can see.

   b) They are nouns that we cannot see. They are emotions.

Exercise 4: Look at the words in boxes and answer the question below.

1. Tom had a │problem│ with his car.

2. I talked to the nurse about the │pain│ in my leg.

3. We finished our │work│ and went home early.

Question: What can we say about these words?

    a) They are nouns that we can see.

    b) They are nouns that we cannot see. They are emotions.

    c) They are not emotions, but they are nouns that we cannot see.

Exercise 5: Circle all the nouns in this paragraph. The number after each sentence indicates the number of nouns in that sentence.

This is a (story) about me.(1) I had a surprise yesterday.(1) It was my birthday, so my parents had a party for me.(3) They invited all my friends, but they didn't tell me.(1) It was a secret.(1) Just before dinner, I arrived home.(2) I opened the door and entered the house.(2) The room was dark, so I turned on the light.(2) My friends jumped up and started to shout.(1) They picked me up in their arms and carried me into the next room.(2) The room had decorations and a table with some food and drinks.(5) They sang a song and gave me some presents.(2) We had a great time.(1)

Exercise 6:   ____1) Fill in the blanks as your teacher reads the sentences.
               ____2) Circle the nouns.

1. Ann _____ a new _____.

2. Some _____ are afraid of _____.

3. A _____ _____ Ken a
    _____.

4. My _____ made _____ for
    _____ _____.

Exercise 7: ___1) Write a paragraph with 5 sentences or more about the topic below.
___2) Circle the nouns.

Topic: Write about what you did yesterday.

Unit 2: Subject Pronouns and Verbs

1. [I] rode the bus to work.
2. [He] hiked to the river.
3. [We] walked through the mall.

Question 1: What do we call the boxed words?

    a) subjects of the sentences (people)

    b) verbs of the sentences (action)

Question 2: What do we call the boxed words?

    a) nouns   b) pronouns   c) verbs

Exercise 2:   Circle the words that can be subjects of a sentence. (There are 5.)

(she)   take   from   (they)   speak

when   (I)   (you)   because   (it)

Exercise 3:   Look at the words in boxes and answer the question below.

1. My friend [is] good at drawing.
2. They [were] too tired to work.
3. Ann [has] a cold.

Question: What can we say about the boxed words?

    a) They are nouns that we cannot see. They are emotions.

    b) They are verbs that show action.

    c) They are verbs that do not show action.

1. (Tom) <u>works</u> in a (factory).
2. That policeman has a great car.
3. Love is important for the world.
4. After the race, the runners were tired.

1. ____ _____ a new CD player.
2. _____ _____ a lot of _____.
3. She _____ happy _____ _____ here.
4. My _____ _____ a pet for her _____.
5. _____ _____ _____ me some medicine.

Topic: Write about some interesting things in your city.

Unit 3: Subjects of Sentences

THE PROBLEM

Is beautiful today.

Exercise 1: Look at the words in boxes and answer the questions below.

1. They | ran | to the park.
2. She | cooked | some spaghetti for dinner.
3. Kenji | speaks | three languages.

Question 1: What do all the words in boxes have in common?

a) They show action.

b) They are things that people can see and touch.

c) They are types of feeling.

Question 2: What do we call the boxed words?

a) nouns

b) pronouns

c) verbs

Exercise 2: Look at the sentence and answer the questions below.

Omar took his TV to the repair shop.

Question 1: What three things can we see and touch in this sentence?

_____, _____, and _____

Question 2: Are these words called nouns or verbs? _____

Question 3: Which word shows action? _____

Question 4: Is that word a noun or a verb? _____

---

1. (Roberto) <u>left</u> early.

Question 1: Who left? _____

2. His computer worked slowly.

Question 2: What worked? _____

3. The cat sat quietly.

Question 3: What sat? _____

Question 4: What do we call the nouns in the sentences above?

a) subjects of the sentences

b) verbs of the sentences

1. The (dishes) <u>fell</u> on the floor.

Question 1: What fell?

a) dishes

b) floor

Question 2: What is the subject of the sentence?

a) The subject of the sentence is *dishes* because it tells us what fell.

b) The subject of the sentence is *floor* because it tells us what fell.

2. Steve drove his car.

Question 3: Who drove?

a) Steve

b) his car

Question 4: What is the subject of the sentence?

a) The subject of the sentence is *car* because it tells us what Steve drove.

b) The subject of the sentence is *Steve* because it tells us who drove.

3. His father bought a pizza for dinner.

Question 5: What is the subject of the sentence?

a) The subject of the sentence is *dinner* because it tells us what bought a pizza.

b) The subject of the sentence is *pizza* because it tells us what bought a pizza.

c) The subject of the sentence is *father* because it tells us who bought a pizza.

4. Tomas is in love with Mimi.

Question 6: What is the subject of the sentence?

a) The subject of the sentence is *Tomas* because it tells who is in love.

b) The subject of the sentence is *Mimi* because it tells us the name of Tomas's lover.

Exercise 5:   ___1) Circle the subjects.
___2) Underline the verbs.
___3) Give the reason for your choice of each subject.

---

1. (He) slept until noon.

Reason: *"He" tells us who slept.*

2. Sam got an interesting haircut.

Reason: _____

3. Amy was happy with her score.

Reason: _____

4. They found the money in the closet.

Reason: _____

Exercise 6: Look at the sentences below.

    ____1) If the sentence has a subject, write *OK*. (3 sentences are OK, including Sentence 2.)

    ____2) If the sentence needs a subject, write a correct sentence.

1. Went to the store.

Tom went to the store.

2. My boss wrote a report.

OK.

3. Gave me a ticket.

_____

4. Were late for our airplane.

_____

5. The dog dug a hole in the yard.

_____

6. Stood in line for the movie.

_____

7. Got an expensive car for his birthday.

_____

8. Is a beautiful day.

_____

9. Ate her dinner at 9 p.m.

_____

10. The passengers are in their seats now.

_____

        S
1. Jane read her book on the couch in the living room for two hours.

2. My bicycle fell in the bushes because of the wind.

3. I got a phone call at midnight.

4. The artist painted a picture of the snow-covered mountains.

Exercise 8:   ___1) Fill in the blanks in these sentences.
               ___2) Write *S* above the subject of each sentence.

1. Last night, _____ watched TV for two hours.

2. My _____ played video games on her
   _____.

3. _____ talked to his _____ on
   the phone.

Exercise 9:   Look at the subjects in these sentences and answer the question below.

        S   *S*
1. My father he is a doctor at a hospital in Seattle.
        S   *S*
2. Good books they are important for our education.

Question: Are these sentences correct?

a) Yes, we can have two subjects, like these, in a sentence.

b) No, we should have only one of these words as the subject.

Exercise 10: Write the 2 sentences in Exercise 9 correctly.

1. _____

2. _____

Exercise 11: ___1) Fill in the blanks as your teacher reads the sentences.
___2) Circle the subjects and underline the verbs.

1. _____ showed us a great _____ _____.

2. _____ _____ is the president of a company.

3. The newspaper _____ a picture of _____ in it.

4. _____ _____ came to my _____ around noon.

Exercise 12: ___1) Write a paragraph with 5 sentences or more about the topic below.
___2) Write *S* above the subjects.

Topic: This is what my _____ did on a recent vacation.
(family/friend/other)

Unit 4: Verbs

THE PROBLEM

She the best worker here.

Exercise 1:   Look at the sentences and answer the questions.

1. Sara drove for eight hours during her trip.

a) What is the subject of the sentence? <u>*Sara*</u>

b) What action did the subject do? <u>*She drove*</u>

2. The child threw his toy in the bathtub.

a) What is the subject of the sentence? _____

b) What action did the subject do? _____

3. I finished my project on time.

a) What is the subject of the sentence? _____

b) What action did the subject do? _____

4. The lazy student told a lie about his homework.

a) What is the subject of the sentence? _____

b) What action did the subject do? _____

Question : What do we call the action words in Exercise 1?

a) subjects

b) verbs

Exercise 2:   Look at the sentences below.
    ____1) If the sentence has a subject and verb, write *OK*.
    ____2) If it needs a verb, write a correct sentence.

1. Tom to the store. <u>*Tom went to the store.*</u>

2. My boss wrote a report. <u>*OK*</u>

3. We the soccer match on TV. _____

4. My sister her dinner at 9 p.m. _____

---

5. We have some old clothes in the basement. _____

_____

6. Amy the piano for an hour. _____

Exercise 3: Write *V* above the verbs.

                    V
1. Amy took a walk to town to buy some supplies.

2. The rain washed all the pollution away.

3. My bank gives us new calendars every January.

4. We learned about mummies at the museum today.

Exercise 4: ___1) Fill in the blanks in the sentences.
              ___2) Write *V* above the verbs.

1. The tourists _____ pictures of the famous sites.

2. The _____ _____ video games until _____ a.m.

3. _____ _____ the bus to work.

Exercise 5: ___1) Fill in the blanks as your teacher reads the sentences.
              ___2) Circle the subjects and underline the verbs.

1. _____ _____ is bird-watching.

2. _____ _____ retired last year.

3. Carlos _____ in an _____ condo.

4. We _____ the four seasons _____ _____ part of Canada.

5. Ann _____ _____ for everyone _____ _____ family.

| Exercise 6: | ___1) Write a paragraph with 5 sentences or more about the topic below. |
| | ___2) Write *V* above the verbs. |

Topic: Write about your childhood.

Unit 5: Grammar Groups Review
Units 1-4

Directions: These sentences and questions are about the worksheet in the box below. Read your sentences and questions to your partners.

1. Look at A. Circle the nouns.
4. Look at B. Write *V* above the verb.
7. Look at D. Write *S* above the subject.
10. Look at F. Should we write the word *he* after the word *brother*? Why or why not?
13. In H, what is the subject?
16. In I, what is the verb?

Worksheet

A. My apartment is near a park.

B. I have a problem with money.

C. There is poverty in many countries.

D. We were happy during the vacation.

E. Have nice weather in summer.

F. My brother quit his job.

G. Cell phones very helpful for police.

H. We played some games at the party.

I. Amy arrived late for our meeting.

J. She some money from the bank.

K. Our boss he gave us too much work to do.

Unit 5: Grammar Groups Review
Units 1-4

Directions: These sentences and questions are about the worksheet in the box below. Read your sentences and questions to your partners.

2. Look at B. Circle the nouns.
5. Look at C. Circle the nouns.
8. In D, write *V* above the verb.
11. Look at G. Is there a problem with this sentence? Explain.
14. Look at I. What is the subject?
17. Look at J. Is there a problem with this sentence? Explain

---

Worksheet

A. My apartment is near a park.

B. I have a problem with money.

C. There is poverty in many countries.

D. We were happy during the vacation.

E. Have nice weather in summer.

F. My brother quit his job.

G. Cell phones very helpful for police.

H. We played some games at the party.

I. Amy arrived late for our meeting.

J. She some money from the bank.

K. Our boss he gave us too much work to do.

Unit 5: Grammar Groups Review
Units 1-4

Directions: These sentences and questions are about the worksheet in the box below. Read your sentences and questions to your partners.

3. In B, write *S* above the subject.

6. In C, did you circle two words?

9. Look at E, is there a problem? If so, how can we correct it?

12. Look at H. What action did the subject do?

15. Look at I. What action did the subject do?

18. Look at K. Is there a problem with this sentence? Explain

---

Worksheet

A. My apartment is near a park.

B. I have a problem with money.

C. There is poverty in many countries.

D. We were happy during the vacation.

E. Have nice weather in summer.

F. My brother quit his job.

G. Cell phones very helpful for police.

H. We played some games at the party.

I. Amy arrived late for our meeting.

J. She some money from the bank.

K. Our boss he gave us too much work to do.

Unit 6:
Be: Auxiliary Verb and Main Verb

THE PROBLEMS

He is wants a dog.
They working too hard.

Exercise 1: ___ 1) Underline the word after *am, is, are, was,* and *were.*
___ 2) Is the underlined word a verb? Write *yes* or *no.*

1. is <u>working</u> hard __*yes*__
2. are <u>in</u> trouble __*no*__
3. are sleeping late _____
4. was listening to _____
5. is a beautiful _____

6. were with us _____
7. were following us _____
8. am going home _____
9. was late because _____
10. am a student here _____

Exercise 2: Fill in the chart with the verbs from Exercise 1.

	Auxiliary Verb	Main Verb
1. is working hard	*is*	*working*
2. are in trouble		*are*
3. are sleeping late		
4. was listening to		
5. is a beautiful		
6. were with us		
7. were following us		
8. am going home		
9. was late because		
10. am a student here		

1. went (V)

2. is sitting (A V)

3. eats

4. are working

5. am riding

6. stopped

7. was visiting

8. is

9. are writing

10. wishes

11. are

12. am watching

13. were showing

14. am

15. is feeling

16. understood

17. was

18. were

19. do

Exercise 4: Choose the correct answers.

1. When the main verb has *-ing*, we _____ an auxiliary verb.
   a) need   b) do not need

2. The words *am, are, is, was,* and *were* _____ .
   a) can be auxiliary verbs   b) can be main verbs   c) can be both

Exercise 5: Write *A* above the auxiliary verbs and *V* above the main verbs. (There are 3 auxiliary verbs.)

1. They are good neighbors.

2. They are visiting their neighbors.

3. I am a musician.

4. Mariko is finishing her second year of college.

5. Ken was making a table for his office.

6. Pedro was in the army for two years.

1. She was starting to make a plan.

a) This verb form is correct. It has an auxiliary verb and a verb+*ing* (*starting*).

b) This verb form is incorrect because it doesn't have an auxiliary verb with a verb+*ing* (*starting*).

2. Steve was a member of the tennis club eight years ago.

a) This verb form is correct because *was* is the main verb of the sentence.

b) This verb form is incorrect because *was* is an auxiliary verb, but there is no main verb.

3. I working for a computer company.

a) This is correct because *working* is the main verb of the sentence.

b) This is incorrect because the verb+*ing* (*working*) needs an auxiliary verb (*am*).

4. Now, Gina is plays soccer at school.

a) This is correct. It has an auxiliary verb (*is*) and a main verb (*plays*) because the subject is *Gina*.

b) This is incorrect because it has an auxiliary verb (*is*) and a main verb (*plays*), but the main verb is not verb+*ing*.

5. We heard some music from our neighbor's apartment.

a) This is correct because *heard* is the main verb of the sentence.

b) This is incorrect because we need an auxiliary verb (*was*) with the main verb (*heard*).

6. Ken buying some presents for his daughter's birthday.

a) This is correct because *buying* is the main verb of the sentence.

b) This is incorrect because it needs an auxiliary verb (*is* or *was*) with the verb+*ing* (*buying*).

7. Joe and Tammy are wash their dirty car today.

a) This is correct. It has an auxiliary verb (*are*) and a main verb (*wash*).

b) This is incorrect because it has an auxiliary verb (*are*) and a main verb (*wash*), but the main verb is not verb+*ing*.

8. Jim in the same class as Julie in elementary school.

a) This is correct because *in* is the main verb of the sentence.

b) This is incorrect because there is no verb in this sentence.

Not OK 1. The author writing a book about my city.

 This sentence needs the auxiliary verb "is."

_____ 2. The girls worked harder than the boys last week.

_____

_____ 3. They are sitting in the garden now.

_____

_____ 4. Tony riding his bicycle to work.

_____

_____ 5. He a man with a lot of hobbies.

_____

Exercise 8:   Correct the mistakes with the verbs in the paragraph. (There are 9
verbs with mistakes, including the 2 corrections.)

                                                        am

1. Last weekend, I ~~am~~ bought a dog, Skip. 2. I ^ building him a
dog house in my back yard, but nowadays, he is sleep in my
house. 3. My other two dogs small, but Skip very big. 4. The three
dogs always running around my yard. 5. They friendly, but Skip
the friendliest. 6. He barking at a cat right now.

1. She _____ an actress.

2. I _____ _____ to say hello.

3. My brother was _____ a report all _____.

4. Our teachers _____ _____ the soccer _____ last night.

5. The workers _____ _____ the problem _____ the _____ now.

Exercise 10:   ___1) Write a paragraph with 5 sentences or more about the topic below.
    ___2) In at least 3 of the sentences, you should have auxiliary verbs.

Topic: Tell us about some interesting friends or members of your family. Explain what they are doing nowadays or what they were doing some time in the past.

Unit 7: Auxiliary Verb Do and Base Verb Forms

THE PROBLEMS

She doesn't likes skiing.
He didn't showed us his painting.
We not know how to drive.

Exercise 1: Circle the correct answers.

1. If you want to look for the definition of the verb *wait* in a dictionary, which form will you look for?

   a) wait   b) waits   c) waiting   d) waited

2. *Wait* is the _____ of the verb.

   a) base or dictionary form   b) *-s* form   c) *-ing* form   d) past tense

3. *Waits* is the _____ of the verb.

   a) base or dictionary form   b) *-s* form   c) *-ing* form   d) past tense

4. *Waiting* is the _____ of the verb.

   a) base or dictionary form   b) *-s* form   c) *-ing* form   d) past tense

5. *Waited* is the _____ of the verb.

   a) base or dictionary form   b) *-s* form   c) *-ing* form   d) past tense

---

Exercise 2: ____1) Write *base* next to the base (dictionary) form of the verbs.
____2) Write *-s* next to the words that are the *-s* form of the verbs.
____3) Write *-ing* next to the words that are the *-ing* form of the verbs.
____4) Write *past* next to the words that are the past tense of the verbs.

1. stay *base*   6. saw _____   11. have _____

2. making *-ing*   7. reading _____   12. liked _____

3. smiles *-s*   8. feels _____   13. drank _____

4. gave *past*   9. carry _____   14. speak _____

5. want _____   10. come _____   15. takes _____

---

1. Luis didn't eat all his vegetables.

2. Did you get the email message that I sent you yesterday?

3. Yuki doesn't enjoy classical music.

4. Do they need tickets?

5. I don't need a ride home tonight.

Question: What do we call the forms of DO in these sentences ? _____
   a) main verbs   b) auxiliary verbs

Exercise 4: Circle the auxiliary and main verbs.

1. His mother (is) (picking) the best vegetables for dinner.

2. Do you always play basketball on the weekends?

3. We didn't need any extra time for the project.

4. She helps some elderly people in their homes.

5. Does Ann have a pet?

6. They save money during summer for college in the fall.

7. I don't like to work on the weekends.

Exercise 5: Fill in the blanks with *make, makes, to make,* or *making.*

Putting *-s* on base verb forms

1. After these subjects: *I, you, we, they, the boys,* and *the cars,* the correct verb form of *make* is _____ .

2. After these subjects: *he, she, it, Sara, Tom,* and *the boy,* the correct verb form of *make* is _____ .

3. After the auxiliary verbs, *do, does, did, don't,* and *didn't,* the correct verb form of *make* is _____ .

Exercise 6: Look at the sentences. Choose the correct explanation for each.

1. He _____ to leave early.

a) We should write *want* because the subject is *he*.

b) We should write *wants* because the subject is *he*.

2. We _____ to leave early.

a) We should write *want* because the subject is *we*.

b) We should write *wants* because the subject is *we*.

3. Ahmed _____ dinner before studying.

a) We should write *eat* because the subject is *Ahmed*.

b) We should write *eats* because the subject is *Ahmed*.

c) We should write *to eats* because the subject is *Ahmed*.

4. It _____ interesting.

a) We should write *look* because the subject is *it*.

b) We should write *looks* because the subject is *it*.

5. These pictures _____ interesting.

a) We should write *look* because the subject is *pictures*.

b) We should write *looks* because the subject is *pictures*.

c) We should write *to look* because the subject is *pictures*.

6. She doesn't _____ winter.

a) We should write *likes* because the subject is *she*.

b) We should write *like* because after *doesn't* we use the base verb form.

7. Sara didn't _____ her report.

a) We should write *finds* because the subject is *she*.

b) We should write *find* because after *didn't* we use the base verb form.

8. Sara and Mari didn't _____ their reports.

a) We should write *finds* because the subjects are *Sara and Mari*.

b). We should write *find* because after *didn't* we use the base verb form.

9. Does Ken _____ a bedroom with his brother?

a) We should write *share* because with the auxiliary verb *does* we use the base verb form.

b) We should write *shares* because the subject is *Ken*.

c) We should write *sharing* because with the auxiliary verb *does* we use verb + *ing*.

1. She _____ home on the weekends.

   a) stay   (b) stays)

   Reason: *We should write "stays" because the subject is "she."*

2. Tom doesn't _____ his bike to work.

   a) ride   b) rides   c) rode

   Reason: _____

3. They didn't _____ their medicine on time.

   a) take   b) takes   c) took

   Reason: _____

4. Gina didn't _____ her medicine on time.

   a) take   b) takes   c) took

   Reason: _____

5. We _____ winter to summer.

   a) prefer   b) prefers

   Reason: _____

6. The teachers didn't _____ my explanation.

   a) understand   b) understands   c) understood

   Reason: _____

7. The workers _____ their best work in the morning.

   a) do   b) does

   Reason: _____

8. They _____ any money in the bank.

   a) not have   b) does not have   c) do not have

   Reason: _____

9. Did you _____ museums during your trip to Europe?

   a) visit   b) visited   c) visiting

   Reason: _____

loves

1. Mary ~~love~~ to run marathons.

2. He <u>didn't forget</u> his passport this time.

3. Toni <u>doesn't</u> summer because it's too hot.

4. We <u>walk</u> two miles every day for exercise.

5. <u>Did</u> they <u>moved</u> to a better apartment?

6. Lee <u>doesn't own</u> any pets.

7. The train <u>come</u> three times an hour.

8. <u>Do</u> they <u>wanting</u> us to make dinner at our house?

9. Hong <u>didn't uses</u> the Internet for her report.

10. My brother <u>not know</u> how to drive a car.

1. My _____ _____ to do tricks.

2. _____ _____ an apple for lunch.

3. _____ _____ _____ the problem.

4. _____ _____ some money to the charity.

5. _____ the _____ _____ his briefcase?

6. Mimi _____ _____ my explanation.

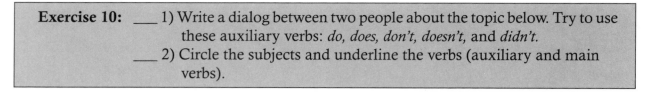

Exercise 10: ___ 1) Write a dialog between two people about the topic below. Try to use these auxiliary verbs: *do, does, don't, doesn't,* and *didn't.*
___ 2) Circle the subjects and underline the verbs (auxiliary and main verbs).

Topic: Two people are talking about the things that their family members like to do and the things that they don't like to do on the weekends. In the dialog, the people ask and answer some questions.

Unit 8: Modals:
Will, Can, Could, Should, Must

THE PROBLEMS

We should to eat vegetables.
They can the hard job quickly.

Exercise 1:   Circle the modals *will, would, can, could, should,* and *must* and underline the verbs after them.

1. Children (should) <u>respect</u> their parents.

2. Ted couldn't open the bottle.

3. Tourists can travel by train around Europe.

4. We mustn't talk during the test.

5. Amy will wash her car before the trip.

Exercise 2:   Choose the correct answers.

---

1. Words such as *will, can, could, should,* and *must* are called _____.
   a) prepositions   b) modals   c) nouns

2. Words such as *will, can, could, should,* and *must* are _____ .
   a) auxiliary verbs   b) main verbs

3. After words such as *will, can, could, should,* and *must*, we use _____.
   a) verb+*ing* (*working*)   b) *to* + verb (*to work*) c) the base verb (*work*)

---

1. Jenny's young son can to count to ten.

a) This sentence is correct. We use *to* + verb (*to count*) after *can*.

b) This sentence is incorrect because we should use the base verb (*count*) after *can*.

2. We couldn't come to the party because of the snow.

a) This sentence is correct. We use the base verb form (*come*) after *couldn't*.

b) This sentence is incorrect because we should use *coming* after *couldn't*.

3. Javier's rent is going up, so he must a part-time job.

a) This sentence is correct. We use *must* as the main verb.

b) This sentence is incorrect because we should use a base verb (such as *find*) after *must*.

4. She should listens to the news more often.

a) This sentence is correct. The subject is *she*, so we put an *-s* at the end of the main verb.

b) This sentence is incorrect because we should use a base verb (*listen*) after *should*.

5. Yesterday, Lora couldn't work because she was tired.

a) This sentence is correct. We use the base verb form (*work*) after *couldn't*.

b) This sentence is incorrect. *Yesterday* is past tense, so we need *worked*, not *work*.

Not OK 1. We can the movie after dinner.

It needs a base verb form after the word "can."

OK 2. Tran should stay in bed because he's sick.

_____

_____ 3. I will helping you soon.

_____

_____ 4. Cindy must write her report again.

_____

_____ 5. My company couldn't made any money this year.

_____

_____ 6. Tomorrow, we should early to start our trip.

_____

_____ 7. Our friends will wait for us in the library.

_____

Exercise 5: Correct the mistakes with modals in the paragraph. (There are 8 mistakes, including *planning*.)

---

1. I recently received information about a group tour that I will join next summer. 2. According to the information, our group should ~~planning~~ *plan* to bring only one suitcase. 3. We must a passport because we will to travel overseas. 4. It is not necessary to have a driver's license, but we could bring one if we want. 5. Because this is a group trip, everyone should to try hard to be on time for the bus departures. 6. Members who are late could causing trouble for everyone. 7. Therefore we should set our alarm clocks every night. 8. At museums, everyone should stayed together. 9. We can to eat lunch alone, but we should our dinner with the group.

Exercise 6: ___1) Fill in the blanks as your teacher reads the sentences.
___2) Circle the verbs (auxiliary and main verbs).

1. Antonio _____ _____ math next quarter.

2. We can _____ _____ fruit at that _____ stand.

3. Next summer I _____ look for ____ new _____.

4. You _____ _____ every _____ for your _____.

5. They _____ yesterday because they _____ find a good _____.

Exercise 7: ___1) Write a paragraph with 5 sentences or more about one   of the topics below.
___2) In at least 3 sentences, use a modal.

Topic Choices: ___1) Explain how to learn a language.

___2) Explain how to buy a good used car.

___3) Explain how to pack for a trip.

Unit 9: Present and Past Tense

THE PROBLEM

Yesterday I go to the library and borrowed a book.

Exercise 1: ___1) Circle the words, *every day, now, yesterday,* and *last week.*
___2) Fill in the blanks with the verbs in the box.
___3) Write the tense of the verb: *present* or *past.*

took   were waiting   ✔give   didn't clean   have
doesn't like   told   are preparing

1. (Every day) we *give* some food to our cat. (*present*)

2. Now they _____ for the celebration.
   (_____)

3. She _____ to get up at 5 a.m., but it's
   necessary. (_____)

4. Every day Melissa's children _____a big breakfast.
   (_____)

5. Last week Anita _____ a trip to Asia. (_____)

6. Yesterday Stefan _____ me about his new job.
   (_____)

7. Last week I _____my room very well, so
   it's messy. (_____)

8. Yesterday Mimi and I _____for you from
   11 a.m. to 1 p.m. (_____)

---

takes ¹·*present*   was watching ²·*past*   wanted ³·_____

is ⁴·_____   doesn't see ⁵·_____   were leaving ⁶·_____

caught ⁷·_____   were ⁸·_____   helps ⁹·_____

is writing ¹⁰·_____   came ¹¹·_____   are ¹²·_____

didn't call ¹³·_____   has ¹⁴·_____   wasn't ¹⁵·_____

Exercise 3:   Choose the correct explanation for each sentence.

1. My brother took me to the mall, and we bought some CDs.

a) This is correct. Both verbs are past tense.

b) This is correct. Both verbs are present tense.

2. Last night, I went to bed at midnight and sleep for eight hours.

a) This is correct. Both verbs are past tense.

b) This is incorrect. One verb is past (*went*), and one verb is present (*sleep*).

3. She is waiting for the mail to arrive because she is hoping to get a letter from her friend.

a) This is correct. Both verbs are present tense.

b) This is incorrect. One verb is past (*is waiting*), and one verb is present (*is hoping*).

4. The plane was late, so we didn't arrive on time

a) This is correct. Both verbs are past tense.

b) This is incorrect. One verb is present (*was*), and one verb is past (*didn't arrive*).

5. Theo felt ill after dinner because he eats some old fish.

a) This is correct. Both verbs are present tense.

b) This is incorrect. One verb is past (*felt*), and one verb is present (*eats*).

6. The kids were hiding outside while Mimi was looking for them.

a) This is correct. Both verbs are past tense.

b) This is incorrect. One verb is past (*were hiding*), and one verb is present (*was looking*).

1. a) Ann shows me the sights of the city, and then we went home.

    b) Ann showed me the sights of the city, and then we go home.

    c) Ann showed me the sights of the city, and then we went home.

2. a) Every day he talks to his uncle on the phone and visits his grandmother.

    b) Every day he talked to his uncle on the phone and visits his grandmother.

    c) Every day he talks to his uncle on the phone and visited his grandmother.

3. a) This year my brother builds a model car because he wanted to give it as a present.

    b) This year my brother is building a model car because he wants to give it as a present.

    c) This year my brother is building a model car because he wanted to give it as a present.

4. a) Last year I go to Europe, but I didn't visit any museums.

    b) Last year I went to Europe, but I didn't visit any museums.

    c) Last year I went to Europe, but I don't visit any museums.

Exercise 5:   Correct the mistakes with verbs. (There are 6 mistakes, including *finds*.)

found

1. Last summer Kenji had a great job. 2. He ~~finds~~ it in the newspaper's help wanted ads. 3. It started at 10 a.m. and ends at 6 p.m., so he had time to go out in the evenings. 4. He never feels tired at work because he was sitting down most of the time. 5.

Unfortunately, he makes mistakes. [6.] His boss didn't want Kenji to send email messages to his friends, but he does. [7.] The boss finds out and fired Kenji.

1. Every day he _____ rice for _____ . (_____)

2. Last week they _____ a park and _____ tennis. (_____)

3. Yesterday I _____ a great _____ , but I _____ _____ it. (_____)

4. Now, Ann _____ _____ for her _____ to finish her piano _____. (_____)

5. Every _____ , we _____ a newspaper and _____ _____ a new apartment. (_____)

Topic: Tell about a surprising experience that happened to you or to someone that you know.

Unit 10: Grammar Groups Review
Units 6-9

Directions: These sentences and questions are about the worksheet in the box below. Read your sentences and questions to your partners.

1. Look at A. Is the word *are* an auxiliary verb or main verb?

4. In C, is there a problem with this verb? Explain.

7. Look at F. Look at the underlined verbs. Circle the correct verb form.

10. Look at H. Underline the verbs.

13. In H, is *meet* present or past tense?

16. In I, what verb tense is the word *was*?

19. In I, are the verb tenses correct?

Worksheet

A. We are living in Bellingham.

B. Sara and Tim are too young to drive.

C. Tom eating lunch in the cafeteria.

D. They are enjoy their classes.

E. He didn't gave me an answer.

F. She doesn't <u>need/needs/needed</u> any help.

G. We were laughing about the joke.

H. I called my friend on the phone and meet her at the mall.

I. Ken was in the same school as me, but we didn't know each other.

J. They will the project before going home.

K. I couldn't <u>open/opening/opened</u> the jar.

Unit 10: Grammar Groups Review
Units 6-9

Directions: These sentences and questions are about the worksheet in the box below. Read your sentences and questions to your partners.

2. Look at B. Is the word *are* an auxiliary verb or main verb?

5. Look at D. Is there a problem with the main verb *enjoy*? Explain.

8. Look at G. Underline the main verb.

11. In H, did you underline two verbs?

14. In H, is there a problem with the verbs? Explain.

17. In I, look at the words *didn't know*. Which is an auxiliary verb and which is a main verb?

20. In J, is there a problem with the verb? Explain.

Worksheet

A. We are living in Bellingham.

B. Sara and Tim are too young to drive.

C. Tom eating lunch in the cafeteria.

D. They are enjoy their classes.

E. He didn't gave me an answer.

F. She doesn't need/needs/needed any help.

G. We were laughing about the joke.

H. I called my friend on the phone and meet her at the mall.

I. Ken was in the same school as me, but we didn't know each other.

J. They will the project before going home.

K. I couldn't open/opening/opened the jar.

Unit 10: Grammar Groups Review
Units 6-9

Directions: These sentences and questions are about the worksheet in the box below. Read your sentences and questions to your partners.

3. Look at C. Underline the verb.

6. Look at E. Should we change the verb *gave*? Explain.

9. In G, is there a problem with the main verb *laughing*? Explain.

12. In H, is *called* present or past tense?

15. Look at I. Underline the verbs.

18. In I, is *didn't know* present or past tense?

21. Look at K. Look at the underlined verbs. Circle the correct verb form.

Worksheet

A. We are living in Bellingham.

B. Sara and Tim are too young to drive.

C. Tom eating lunch in the cafeteria.

D. They are enjoy their classes.

E. He didn't gave me an answer.

F. She doesn't <u>need/needs/needed</u> any help.

G. We were laughing about the joke.

H. I called my friend on the phone and meet her at the mall.

I. Ken was in the same school as me, but we didn't know each other.

J. They will the project before going home.

K. I couldn't <u>open/opening/opened</u> the jar.

Unit 11: Clauses and Compound Sentences

THE PROBLEMS

He felt ill he went to the doctor.
He felt ill, he went to the doctor.

Part 1: Identify sentences and clauses.

Exercise 1: Circle the groups of words that can be complete sentences. (You should have 8 circles, including the 2 in Sentence 1.)

1. (he turned off the light,) (he went to bed)

2. we took a tour of the castle it was very scary

3. Carrie parked the car, she put money in the meter

4. the train was late we got home after midnight

Exercise 2: Choose the correct answer.

The 8 circled groups of words in Exercise 1 above can be sentences.
Groups of words that can be sentences are called _____ because
they have a subject and a verb.

      a) clauses   b) subjects   c) auxiliaries

Exercise 3: Choose the groups of words that are clauses. Remember, a clause has a subject and verb. (There are 3 clauses.)

_____ 1. in the morning

_____ 2. he bought a new computer

_____ 3. my best friend from Europe

_____ 4. loud music hurts my ears

____ 5. she feels homesick

____ 6. a wonderful and beautiful picture

____ 7. is fun to do sports

1. a. (I talked to my friend for an hour)(we laughed a lot.)

   b. (I talked to my friend for an hour.)(We laughed a lot.)

2. a. It was snowing. We drove slowly.

   b. It was snowing we drove slowly.

3. a. Sara speaks French she doesn't understand Chinese.

   b. Sara speaks French. She doesn't understand Chinese.

4. a. The lion chased the deer, she didn't catch it.

   b. The lion chased the deer. She didn't catch it.

5. a. The sky looked stormy. Everyone stayed inside.

   b. The sky looked stormy, everyone stayed inside.

Part 2: Combine clauses with conjunctions.

1. a. (My father paid the bill)(we went home.)

   b. (My father paid the bill,) and (we went home.)

2. a. Steve needs to save money, he doesn't have a job.

   b. Steve needs to save money, but he doesn't have a job.

3. a. I gave a speech yesterday, and it was fun.

   b. I gave a speech yesterday it was fun.

4. a. The movie ended at midnight, so we got home late.

   b. The movie ended at midnight. We got home late.

   c. The movie ended at midnight, we got home late.

5. a. Jay's favorite actor made a new movie. He plans to see it soon.

   b. Jay's favorite actor made a new movie he plans to see it soon.

   c. Jay's favorite actor made a new movie, and he plans to see it soon.

Exercise 6:   Choose the correct answers.

The words *and, but,* and *so* are called [1.] _____.
   a) conjunctions   b) clauses   c) subjects
We use the words *and, but,* and *so* to connect two [2.] _____.
   a) conjunctions   b) clauses   c) subjects

Exercise 7:   Look at the sentences. Choose the correct explanation for each. (There are 7 correct ones.)

---

1. He had an appointment, so he left school early.

a) This sentence is correct because we connected two clauses with *so*.

b) This sentence is incorrect because we need a period before *so*.

2. They were invited to a party, but they didn't go.

a) This sentence is correct because we connected two clauses with *but*.

b) This sentence is incorrect because we need a period before *but*.

---

3. We will eat lunch at noon. We'll have dinner at eight.

a) These sentences are correct.

b) These sentences are correct, but we could combine them by adding: comma + *and*.

c) These sentences are incorrect. We could take out the period and put a small *w* on *We'll*.

4. This hair-dryer doesn't work he needs a new one.

a) This sentence is correct.

b) This sentence is incorrect. We could put a period after *work* and capitalize *he*.

c) This sentence is incorrect. After *work*, we could add: comma + *so*.

5. My father gave me a car, but it too old.

a) This sentence is correct.

b) This sentence is incorrect. We should put a period after *car* and capitalize *but*.

c) This sentence is incorrect. After the word *it*, we should add the verb *is*.

Exercise 8:   ___1) Write *OK* if the sentences are correct. (2 are correct.)
___2) Add periods and capitals, or add conjunctions (*and, but, so*) to make correct sentences.

___ 1. I like birds I want to fly like one.

___ 2. Ann had to give a speech, so she was nervous.

___ 3. We went to the beach the water was too cold to swim.

___ 4. My guitar string broke. Ken gave me his guitar to use.

___ 5. Sara is coming after work Tami will arrive as soon as possible.

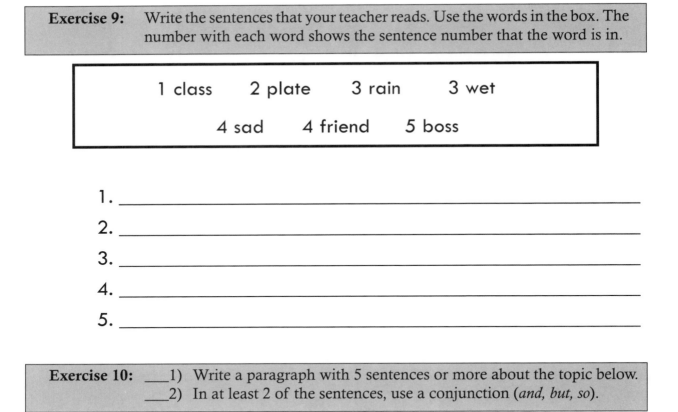

1 class   2 plate   3 rain   3 wet

4 sad   4 friend   5 boss

1. _____

2. _____

3. _____

4. _____

5. _____

Exercise 10: ____1) Write a paragraph with 5 sentences or more about the topic below.
____2) In at least 2 of the sentences, use a conjunction (*and, but, so*).

Topic: Write about things that you did as a child (7-12 years old). You can include things that you enjoyed and did not enjoy.

Unit 12: Prepositions

THE PROBLEMS

Jon is in the phone.
The man near the cars are my neighbor.

```
        D
    B | E |   A           F
        C
```

1. ____ is above the box.

2. ____ is next to or beside the box.

3. ____ is in or inside the box.

4. ____ is near the box, and _____ is far from the box.

5. ____ is below the box.

1. My house is (near) a mall.

2. There is a great Asian restaurant in our neighborhood.

3. Under his car, you will find a small pool of oil.

4. My brother rented an apartment near me, so I can eat dinner with him now.

to	about	in	of	during
with	at	from	for	

1. Ken left early _____ the morning.

2. My friend is traveling to Asia _____ his wife.

3. They went _____ the party, but they didn't enjoy it.

4. We waited _____ an hour, and then we went back home.

5. She got a letter _____ her pen pal.

6. _____ nine o'clock, the alarm rang, so everyone ran outside.

7. Don told me _____ his problem.

8. Jan is tired _____ work, but she can't quit yet.

9. The students watched a movie _____ class.

Exercise 4: Choose the correct answers.

1. After a preposition, we need a _____ .
   a) noun   b) verb   c) clause   d) preposition

2. A preposition with a noun after it is called _____.
   a) a prepositional clause because it has a noun and verb.
   b) a prepositional phrase because it has a noun, but it doesn't have a verb.

3. After a preposition, we can have _____ .
   a) a one-word noun (for example, *work*)
   b) a noun phrase (for example, *the morning*)
   c) both (a one-word noun *or* a noun phrase)

1. In Alaska, it often snows during winter.

a) This is correct. There is a preposition (*during*) followed by a noun (*winter*).

b) This is not correct. There is a preposition (*during*) but *winter* is not a noun. It's a verb.

2. My parents are proud my essay.

a) This is correct. There is a preposition (*my*) followed by a noun (*essay*).

b) This is not correct. We need a preposition (*of*) before the noun phrase (*my essay*).

3. In our city, we can find many interesting buildings.

a) This is correct. There is a preposition (*in*) followed by a noun phrase (*our city*).

b) This is not correct. We cannot start a sentence with a prepositional phrase.

4. From his father learned how to drive a car.

a) This is correct. There is a preposition (*from*) followed by a noun phrase (*his father*).

b) This is not correct. The prepositional phrase (*from his father*) is correct. The sentence has a verb (*learned*) but no subject. We need a subject (such as *Jim*) in the sentence.

5. Tom lives in a small house near a river.

a) This is correct. There is a preposition (*in*) followed by a noun phrase (*a small house*) and a second preposition (*near*) followed by a noun phrase (*a river*).

b) This is not correct. We cannot have two prepositional phrases (*in a small house* and *near a river*) in one sentence.

6. At my college are many students.

a) This is correct. There is a preposition (*at*) followed by a noun phrase (*my college*).

b) This is not correct. The prepositional phrase (*at my college*) is correct, but there is no subject in this sentence.

1. We searched (for) <u>a gift</u> all morning.
2. They found the lost dog in the forest.
3. Sara went shopping for a used car.
4. During summer, Ken had a part-time job.
5. The team usually travels by bus.
6. They had a good time with their friends at the party.

Exercise 7: ____1) Write the sentences that your teacher reads. Use the words in the box. The number with each word shows the sentence number that the word is in.
____2) Circle the prepositions. (There are 6.)

1 meeting	2 program	3 suitcase
4 cell phone	4 plan	

1. _____

2. _____

3. _____

4. _____

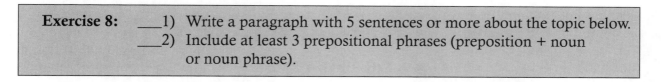

Exercise 8: ___1) Write a paragraph with 5 sentences or more about the topic below.

___2) Include at least 3 prepositional phrases (preposition + noun or noun phrase).

Topic: Write about a trip that you took.

Unit 13: Non-Referential IT

THE PROBLEMS

Was raining after work.
He is easy to do math.

Exercise 1: Write the meaning of the word *it* in each sentence.

1. I saw a dog. It was black. (*It* is the _dog._)

2. The house was brand new. It cost about $150,000.

(*It* is the _____.)

3. We bought a car, but it was very slow.

(*It* is the _____.)

4. Sara couldn't find her hat. It was her favorite one.

(*It* is the _____.)

Exercise 2: Choose one of the words in the box to identify the situation of each sentence.

temperature	weather	time	distance

time 1. It is 3 o'clock.

_____ 2. It is about ten miles to the next gas station.

_____ 3. It is sunny today.

_____ 4. It is 40° outside.

_____ 5. It's raining.

_____ 6. It's 8:30.

---

1. I need to put on a coat. It is freezing outside.

a) *It* refers to *coat*.

b) We don't know the specific word that *It* refers to.

2. She decided to go to bed because it was almost midnight.

a) *It* refers to bed.

b) We don't know the specific word that *it* refers to.

1. In Exercise 1 above (for example: *I saw a dog. It was black.*), we _____ the specific word that *it* refers to.

    a) know   b) do not know

2. In Exercise 1 above, *it* is called _____ because it refers to a specific word.

    a) referential *it*   b) non-referential *it*

3. In Exercises 2 and 3 above (for example: *It is 3 o'clock.*), we _____ the specific word that *it* refers to.

    a) know   b) do not know

4. In Exercises 2 and 3 above, *it* is called _____ because it does not refer to a specific word.

    a) referential *it*   b) non-referential *it*

1. We went home early because it was getting cold. *none*

2. Ken took a taxi to the airport. It cost about $25. *taxi*

3. When she left work, it was 3:30. _____

4. There was a storm last night. It caused some problems.

   _____

5. It's too windy, so let's stay home tonight. _____

6. I decided not to buy my neighbor's house since it was so old.

   _____

7. Is it about 1,000 miles from New York to Chicago? _____

1. It is <u>pretty</u> in spring in my hometown.

2. It's crowded in the airport during the holidays.

3. Tom couldn't finish his work because it was late.

4. He practiced his song for three weeks, so it was easy for him to perform.

Question: What kind of word is underlined above?

    a) noun   b) adjective   c) verb

Not OK 1. Ken started to sweat because ^*it* was hot outside.

Not OK 2. ~~Steve is easy~~ *It is easy for Steve* to use a computer.

_____ 3. It's sad that he can't find a good job.

_____ 4. Jane got a headache because she was hard to write her report.

_____ 5. I am difficult to drive in the city.

_____ 6. The picnic was a success because it was warm and sunny.

_____ 7. Is a good idea to get eight hours of sleep at night.

_____ 8. We couldn't find a seat because it crowded in the theater.

Exercise 8: Write the sentences that your teacher reads. Use the words in the box. The number with each word shows the sentence number that the word is in.

1 movie	2 necessary	2 airport
3 minutes	3 mall	4 friends

1. _____

2. _____

3. _____

4. _____

1. Write two sentences with referential *it*.

_____

_____

2. Write two sentences with non-referential *it*.

_____

_____

3. Write sentences with these words:

It is difficult   **Is it easy**

It isn't necessary   **It was impossible**

_____

_____

_____

_____

Unit 14: There and Their

THE PROBLEMS

I like there house.
Their is some water in our garage.

Exercise 1: ___1) Look at the sentences.
___2) Choose the answers about *there* and *their* in the box below.

1. They enjoyed their vacation in Bali.

2. They always go there during the winter.

3. There is great hotel on the beach.

4. Their room had a view of the ocean.

5. There is a carpet in the room.

6. It usually rains in the afternoon there.

---

1. After the word _____, we have a noun.
   a) *their*   b) *there*
2. After the word _____, we do not have a noun.
   a) *their*   b) *there*

Exercise 2: Look at the sentences. Choose the correct explanation for each.

1. Dan and Jill are happy because there office has a view of the mountains.

a) This is correct. After the word *there*, we need a noun (*office*).

b) This is incorrect. We should use the word *their* because a noun (*office*) follows it.

2. Sara and Ken worked in their garden all day.

a) This is correct. After the word *their*, we have a noun (*garden*).

b) This is incorrect. We should use the word *there* because a noun (*garden*) follows it.

---

3. We left there at noon.

(a) This is correct. After the word *there*, we do not have a noun.

b) This is incorrect. We should use the word *their* because a noun *(at)* follows it.

4. There is some cake for dessert.

(a) This is correct. After the word *there*, we do not have a noun. We have a verb *(is)*.

b) This is incorrect. We should put a noun after *there*.

5. It's very dangerous, so you shouldn't go there.

(a) This is correct. After the word *there*, we do not have a noun.

b) This is incorrect. We should use *their* at the end of a sentence.

Exercise 3:   Choose the letter of the mistake. (There is only one.)

a) Jose's book

b) his book

c) our book

d) my book

e) Ann's book

f) her book

g) Sara's book

(h) there book

i) their book

Exercise 4:   ___1) Write *OK* if the sentence is correct. (4 sentences are OK.)
___2) If the sentence is incorrect, correct the mistake.

Their
___ 1. ~~There~~ dog is not trained well.

OK 2. There is a train at noon today.

___ 3. I'm embarrassed because I forgot to go there.

                                              their
___ 4. The children got a present for ~~there~~ parents.

---

there

____ 5. Tell me if their is a problem with my answer.

_OK_ 6. Why don't you want to go there for dinner?

_OK_ 7. Their weekend was wonderful.

_OK_ 8. There is a great movie on TV tonight.

Exercise 5:   Write the sentences that your teacher reads. Use the words in the box. The number with each word shows the sentence number that the word is in.

---

1 winter   2 workers   3 project   4 opinions

5 autobiographies   6 newspaper

---

1. _____

2. _____

3. _____

4. _____

5. _____

6. _____

Exercise 6:   Write 2 sentences with each of these words: *there* and *their*. (You should write a total of 4 sentences.)

Unit 15: Grammar Groups Review
Units 11-14

Directions: These sentences and questions are about the worksheet in the box below. Read your sentences and questions to your partners.

1. Look at A. Draw a circle around the clauses.
4. Look at B. Put in capitals and periods.
7. Look at D. Put in a capital letter and periods.
10. Look at G. Circle the prepositions.
13. In H, did you circle four prepositions?
16. Look at K. Is there a problem with the word *there*?

Worksheet

A. my grandfather made this table it's an antique now

B. she wanted to visit you at the hospital but she was too busy

C. He is easy to fix computers.

D. The author wrote a book it became popular

E. Ken enjoys tennis, so he usually plays on weekends.

F. Ann wanted to ski, she didn't go because there was no snow.

G. •at •early •to •his •so •for •of •is •with •below •can •from

H. We stayed at a resort in the mountains near a ranch with horses.

I. He looked his watch to see the time.

J. They put there new piano in the living room.

K. There is no school today because of the storm.

L. The family showed their new car to the neighbors.

Unit 15: Grammar Groups Review
Units 11-14

STUDENT B

Directions: These sentences and questions are about the worksheet in the box below. Read your sentences and questions to your partners.

2. In A, put in capitals and periods.

5. In B, did you put in only one capital and one period?

8. Look at E. Is there a problem with this sentence? Explain.

11. In G, did you circle seven words?

14. Look at I. This sentence needs a preposition. Add it.

17. Look at L. Is there a problem with the word *their*? Explain.

Worksheet

A. my grandfather made this table it's an antique now

B. she wanted to visit you at the hospital but she was too busy

C. He is easy to fix computers.

D. The author wrote a book it became popular

E. Ken enjoys tennis, so he usually plays on weekends.

F. Ann wanted to ski, she didn't go because there was no snow.

G. •at •early •to •his •so •for •of •is •with •below •can •from

H. We stayed at a resort in the mountains near a ranch with horses.

I. He looked his watch to see the time.

J. They put there new piano in the living room.

K. There is no school today because of the storm.

L. The family showed their new car to the neighbors.

Unit 15: Grammar Groups Review
Units 11-14

Directions: These sentences and questions are about the worksheet in the box below. Read your sentences and questions to your partners.

3. Look at B. Draw circles around the clauses.

6. Look at C. Is there a problem with the subject? Explain.

9. Look at F. Is there a problem with this sentence? Explain.

12. Look at H. Circle the prepositions.

15. Look at J. Is there a problem with the word *there*? Explain.

Worksheet

A. my grandfather made this table it's an antique now

B. she wanted to visit you at the hospital but she was too busy

C. He is easy to fix computers.

D. The author wrote a book it became popular

E. Ken enjoys tennis, so he usually plays on weekends.

F. Ann wanted to ski, she didn't go because there was no snow.

G. •at •early •to •his •so •for •of •is •with •below •can •from

H. We stayed at a resort in the mountains near a ranch with horses.

I. He looked his watch to see the time.

J. They put there new piano in the living room.

K. There is no school today because of the storm.

L. The family showed their new car to the neighbors.

Unit 16: Because and Since

THE PROBLEMS

Because it was raining.
Because I'm late, so I'll take a taxi.
Since he has a problem.

Exercise 1: Circle the clauses. Remember from Unit 11, a clause has a subject and verb. (There are 10 clauses, including the 2 in Sentence 1.)

1. (I bought an airline ticket) because (I want to visit my uncle.)

2. Since our dog was sick, we took it to the vet.

3. Since Mari didn't speak English, she spoke French to the shop-keeper.

4. The mailman was late today because it was snowing so hard.

5. Because the air conditioner broke, all classes were canceled.

Exercise 2: Choose the correct answers.

---

1. According to the sentences in Exercise 1, when we use *because* or *since* in a sentence, we have ___.

   a) one clause   b) two clauses

2. When we use *Because* or *Since* at the beginning of a sentence, we usually _____ a comma after the first clause.

   a) use   b) do not use

Note: *Since* can also be a preposition, as in *It has been raining since 3 o'clock.*

Exercise 3: Look at the sentences. Choose the correct explanation for each.

1. I went to the library because I needed a book for my report.

a) This sentence with *because* is correct because it has two clauses.

b) This sentence with *because* is incorrect because it has only one clause.

2. Because I was very lucky.

a) This sentence with *because* is correct because it has two clauses.

b) This sentence with *because* is incorrect because it has only one clause.

3. Since my country had elections yesterday, we had a holiday.

a) This sentence with *since* is correct because it has two clauses.

b) This sentence with *since* is incorrect because it has only one clause.

4. The workers look happy today. Because they got their pay-checks.

a) These sentences are correct because they are two clauses.

b) The first sentence is correct, but the second one with *because* is incorrect because it has only one clause.

5. Since the roof is beginning to leak, we need a new one.

a) This sentence with *since* is correct because it has two clauses.

b) This sentence with *since* is incorrect because it has only one clause.

6. Because the child was scared. She started crying.

a) These sentences are correct because they are two clauses.

b) The first sentence is incorrect because it has only one clause with *because*. The second sentence is correct.

Exercise 4: Choose the correct answer.

A clause that starts with the word *because* or *since* is called ___ .

a) a dependent clause because it needs a second clause in the sentence.
   In other words, it cannot stand alone.

b) an independent clause because it can be a sentence without a second clause.
   In other words, it can stand alone.

1. a) Because he is tired, so he wants to go home.
   b) Because he is tired, ~~so~~ he wants to go home.
2. a) Since Tom plays the piano, ~~and~~ he will perform at our party.
   b) Since Tom plays the piano, and he will perform at our party.

Exercise 6: Choose the correct answer.

> When we use *because* or *since* at the start of a sentence, we usually _____ the words *so* and *and* in the second clause.
> a) use   b) do not use

Exercise 7:   ___1) Write *OK* if the sentences are correct. (3 sentences are OK, including Sentence 1.)
        ___2) Correct the sentences if they are incorrect.

_OK_ 1. Ken didn't have many friends in elementary school because he was shy.

____ 2. My parents bought me a new computer. ~~Because~~ *because* I passed my math class.

____ 3. We moved to the city because my father found a great job there.

____ 4. Since my brother was sick. We called Dr. Wilson.

____ 5. Because we won the game, so we will go to a restaurant to celebrate.

____ 6. Since they took a lot of pictures of their vacation. They have many nice memories.

____ 7. Because she was a teenager, and she wanted to have her own bedroom.

____ 8. I started to cry at the end of the book. Because the ending was very sad.

____ 9. Since the movie was boring, Sara fell asleep.

Write the sentences that your teacher reads. Use the words in the box. The number with each word shows the sentence number that the word is in.

1 library	2 fire station	3 invitation
	3 party	4 midnight

1. _____

2. _____

3. _____

4. _____

Exercise 9: ____1) Write a paragraph with 5 sentences or more about one of the topics below.

____2) In at least 3 of the sentences, use *because* or *since*.

Topic Choices: ____1) Write about what you did last weekend and why you did it.

____2) Write about your plans for next weekend and why you will do them.

Unit 17:
Have: Auxiliary and Main Verb

THE PROBLEMS

He have a new suit.
They not finished yet.

Exercise 1: ___1) Write *A* above the auxiliary verbs. (There are 5 auxiliary verbs, including Number 2.)
___2) Write *V* above the main verbs.

V
1. have

A V
2. has started

3. have lived

4. haven't eaten

5. has

6. has worked

7. hasn't seen

Exercise 2: ___1) Write *A* above the auxiliary verbs. (There are 8 auxiliary verbs including *have* in Number 2.)
___2) Write *V* above the main verbs.

V
1. We have a swimming pool in our back yard.

A   V
2. They have already seen that movie.

3. Debbie has never had a pet.

4. He hasn't had his exam yet.

5. Yuri has been in his apartment since July.

6. You have never called me on your cell phone.

7. I have a list of jobs for you.

8. My uncle has two tickets for the basketball game.

9. We have lived here for a year.

10. She has slept for two hours.

11. Ann hasn't ever played a computer game.

Exercise 3: ____1) Look at the sentences in Exercise 2 above and underline the words *already, ever, yet, since, never,* and *for.*
____2) Choose the correct answers below.

1. With the words *already, ever, yet, since,* and *never,* we _____ the auxiliary verb *has* or *have.*

   a) need   b) do not need

2. The words *has* and *have* ____.

   a) can be auxiliary verbs   b) can be main verbs

   c) can be both auxiliary verbs and main verbs

Exercise 4: Write the time expressions from Sentences 9 and 10 in Exercise 2 above.

9. *for* ____ _____

10. *for* _____ _____

Exercise 5: ____1) Look at Sentences 7-10 in Exercise 2 above.
____2) Choose the correct answers below.

3. Sentences which have the word *for* in them _____ the auxiliary verb *has* or *have.*

   a) always need   b) do not need   c) sometimes need

4. When we use *for* + a time expression, we _____ the auxiliary verb *has* or *have.*

   a) need   b) do not need

1. She have a lot of vegetables in her garden.

a) This is correct. It has a main verb (*have*).

b) This is incorrect. After the word *she*, we use *has*.

2. Celine has already her assignments.

a) This is correct. It has a main verb (*has*).

b) This is incorrect. With the word *already*, we need an auxiliary verb (*has*) and a main verb (such as *finished*).

3. They have bought videos at the store on the corner since 1999.

a) This is correct. Because it has *since* + a time expression *(1999)*, it has an auxiliary verb (*have*) and main verb (*bought*).

b) This is incorrect. We need only the main verb (*bought*). We don't need an auxiliary verb (*have*).

4. My brother hasn't taken a driver's test yet.

a) This is correct. Because it has the word *yet*, it has an auxiliary verb (*hasn't*) and main verb (*taken*).

b) This is incorrect. We need only the main verb (*taken*). We don't need an auxiliary verb (*hasn't*).

5. I have been on a diet for three months.

a) This is correct. It needs an auxiliary verb (*have*) and main verb (*been*), because it has *for* + a time expression (*three months*).

b) This is incorrect. Because *three months* is not a time expression after *for*, we need only a main verb, *was*, not *have been*.

6. We have a good idea for our project.

a) This is correct. It needs only a main verb (*have*) because *our project* is not a time expression.

b) This is incorrect. Because it has the word *for*, it needs an auxiliary verb (*have*) and main verb (such as *had*).

7. That man has talked on his cell phone for 25 minutes.

a) This is correct. It needs an auxiliary verb (*has*) and main verb (*talked*), because it has *for* +a time expression (*25 minutes*).

b) This is incorrect. Because *25 minutes* is not a time phrase after *for*, we need only a main verb (*talked*).

8. Olga has some medicine for her illness.

a) This is correct. It needs only a main verb (*has*) because *her illness* is not a time expression.

b) This is incorrect. Because it has the word *for*, it needs an auxiliary verb (*has*) and main verb (such as *bought*).

Exercise 7: Look at the sentences. Choose the correct explanation for each.

1. They finish their homework every day at home.

   Explanation: We use _____ because the sentence is in the present tense.
   a) an auxiliary and main verb   b) just a main verb

2. They have already finished their homework.

   Explanation: We use _____ because the sentence has *already* in it.
   a) an auxiliary and main verb   b) just a main verb

3. They have already finished their homework.

   Explanation: The verb tense of the verb (*have finished*) is called _____ tense.
   a) present   b) present perfect

4. Sara hasn't eaten dinner yet.

   Explanation: The verb (*hasn't eaten*) is _____ tense.
   a) present   b) present perfect

5. Joni doesn't have enough gas in her car.

   Explanation: The verb (*doesn't have*) is _____ tense.
   a) present   b) present perfect

6. Lee has dinner at 6 p.m. every night.

   Explanation: The verb (*has*) is _____ tense.
   a) present   b) present perfect

7. Mimi has money for college.

   Explanation: The verb (*has*) is _____ tense.
   a) present   b) present perfect

8. I have thought about the problem for two weeks.

   Explanation: The verb (*have thought*) is _____ tense.
   a) present   b) present perfect

Exercise 8: ___1) Next to each verb, write the verb tense: *past* or *pres perf*.
___2) If the verb tense is present perfect, underline the auxiliary verb and circle the main verb.

*past*_____1. lived   *pres perf*___ 2. has (lived)

_____ 3. have seen   _____ 4. saw

_____ 5. worked   _____ 6. have worked

_____ 7. went   _____ 8. have gone

_____ 9. have made   _____ 10. made

Exercise 9: Choose the correct answers.

1. Present perfect tense has _____
   a) a main verb only   b) an auxiliary and main verb
2. In present perfect tense, the main verb is _____ the past tense form.
   a) always the same as   b) sometimes different from
3. In present perfect tense, the main verb is called a _____
   a) subject   b) noun   c) past participle

Exercise 10: Circle the past participles. (There are 6, including *written*.)

1. I haven't (written) the apology yet.

2. Ken has never played tennis.

3. We understood the lecture clearly.

4. She always goes shopping during the holidays.

5. That man has lived in this neighborhood since 1962.

6. Have you ever seen a ghost?

7. Jan has already bought all the software.

8. We haven't been in this room very long.

Exercise 11: Fill in the chart with the words in the box.

began	is	driven	wrote	went
seen	give	eat	taken	am
given	took	written	saw	been
	are		drive	

Base Form	Simple Past	Past Participle
1. go	_____	gone
2. _____	ate	eaten
3. _____	gave	_____
4. see	_____	_____
5. ___ / ___ / ___	was / were	_____
6. begin	_____	begun
7. _____	drove	_____
8. write	_____	_____
9. take	_____	_____

Exercise 12: Fill in the blanks with verbs from the chart in Exercise 11. Then explain why you chose that form.

1. They have already _begun_ to pack for their trip.

   Reason: _We use the past participle with "have" and "already."_

   _____

2. Jim doesn't have a driver's license, so he hasn't _____ a car yet.

   Reason: _____

   _____

3. Sara has _____ in this city since 2001.

   Reason: _____

   _____

4. My brother is only ten years old, but he has already _____ to many foreign countries.

   Reason: _____

   _____

5. The president has never _____ a speech in our city.

   Reason: _____

   _____

6. Have you ever _____ an essay in a foreign language?

   Reason: _____

   _____

Exercise 13: ____ 1) Write the sentences that your teacher reads. Use the words in the box. The number with each word is the sentence number for that word.

____ 2) After each sentence, write *present* if the verb is in the present tense and *pres perf* if it is present perfect.

1 uncle	2 sign	3 employees
4 bought	4 post office	5 early

1. _____ (_____)

2. _____ (_____)

3. _____ (_____)

4. _____ (_____)

5. _____ (_____)

Exercise 14: Write sentences and use one of the words below in each sentence. You should have 7 sentences.

already	since	yet	every day	now
for (+ a time expression)			never	

Unit 18: Present Perfect Tense vs. Past Tense

THE PROBLEMS

She has lived there last year.
They didn't call yet.

Exercise 1: ____1) Circle the verbs (auxiliary verbs, main verbs and past participles).
____2) Write *past* if the verb is in the past tense and *pres perf* if the verb is in the present perfect tense.

---

1. I (had) a problem with my computer yesterday. *past*

2. We (have) already (seen) that movie. *pres perf*

3. Sami has never hiked to the top of a mountain. _____

4. They were in the basement during the storm. _____

5. Lee has been late every day since Monday. _____

6. Many people cried at the end of the movie. _____

7. Ann didn't wait for me at the station. _____

8. I haven't begun my homework yet. _____

Exercise 2: Look at the sentences and complete the explanations.

1. They finished their homework very late last night.

Explanation: We use _____ because the sentence is in the past tense.
  a) an auxiliary and past participle   b) just a main verb

2. He hasn't slept at all for two nights.

Explanation: We use _____ because the sentence is in the present perfect tense.
  a) an auxiliary and past participle   b) just a main verb

3. The passengers have already started to board the plane.

Explanation: We use _____ because the sentence is in the present perfect tense.
  a) an auxiliary and main verb   b) an auxiliary and past participle

---

4. My boss didn't like my excuse.

Explanation: We use _____ because the sentence is in the past tense.

    a) an auxiliary and main verb   b) an auxiliary verb and past participle

5. The bank opens at 9 a.m. every day except weekends.

Explanation: The verb (*opens*) is in the _____ tense.

    a) present   b) present perfect   c) past

6. Antonio's father has never forgotten his birthday.

Explanation: The verb (*has forgotten*) is in the _____ tense.

    a) present   b) present perfect   c) past

7. Sara ate dinner at 6 p.m. last night.

Explanation: The verb (*ate*) is in the _____ tense.

    a) present   b) present perfect   c) past

Exercise 3:   Write the verb tense for each verb. Use *present, present perfect,* and *past.*

present	1. calls	*past*	2. called
pres perf	3. has called	_____	4. lived
_____	5. have lived	_____	6. live
_____	7. has built	_____	8. builds
_____	9. built	_____	10. drinks
_____	11. drank	_____	12. has drunk
_____	13. don't make	_____	14. didn't make
_____	15. haven't made		

Base Form	Present Tense	Past Tense	Present Perfect Tense
clean	He _cleans_	He _cleaned_	He _has cleaned_
play	He _____	He _____	He _____
play	We _____	We _____	We _____
sit	I _____	I _____	I _____
teach	You _____	You _____	You _____
buy	She doesn't ____	She didn't ____	She hasn't _____
live	They _____	They _____	They _____
write	I don't _____	I didn't _____	I haven't _____
eat	He _____	He _____	He _____
give	We _____	We _____	We _____
have	You _____	You _____	You _____
travel	They _____	They _____	They _____
take	She doesn't ____	She didn't ____	She hasn't _____

Exercise 5:   Fill in the blanks with verbs from the chart in Exercise 4 and explain why you chose them.

1. Yesterday, I _cleaned_ my messy bedroom.

Reason: _We use simple past with "yesterday."_

2. Mari _has sat_ at her computer since 8 o'clock.

Reason: _We use present perfect with "since" and a time expression._

3. We _didn't write_ a letter to the newspaper.

Reason: _We use the base form after "didn't."_

4. Last year, they _____ around the world.

Reason: _____

5. Jim doesn't have much money, so he _____ a car yet.

Reason: _____

6. Now, Maria_____ in the suburbs, but she works in the city.

Reason: _____

7. Mr. Todd and Ms. Smith _____ math at this university for eight years.

Reason: _____

8. The students _____ a break during the test last Friday.

Reason: _____

9. In France in 1999, Patti _____ a lot of bread and cheese.

Reason: _____

10. My boss _____ never _____ me a present on my birthday.

Reason: _____

11. Ken _____ video games for several hours.

Reason: _____

12. I didn't finish my report because I _____ a problem with my computer.

Reason: _____

Exercise 6: Choose the correct answers.

1. Present perfect tense has _____.
   a) a main verb only   b) an auxiliary and past participle
2. In present perfect tense, the past participle is _____ the past tense form.
   a) always the same form as b) sometimes a different form from

1. We had a good time at Jim's party last weekend.

a) This is correct. It has a main verb (*had*) for past tense.

b) This is incorrect. With the words *last weekend*, we need an auxiliary verb (*has*) and a past participle (*had*).

2. Every summer, they take a trip to the mountains for their vacation.

a) This is correct. It has a main verb (*take*) in the present tense.

b) This is incorrect. With the expression, *Every summer*, we need an auxiliary verb (*have*) and a main verb (*taken*).

3. Tom never saw a zebra.

a) This is correct. It has a main verb (*saw*) for past tense.

b) This is incorrect. With the word *never*, we need an auxiliary verb (*has*) and past participle (*seen*).

4. I haven't spoke to my boss about my pay raise yet.

a) This is correct. With the word *yet,* we need an auxiliary verb (*haven't*) and a main verb (*spoke*).

b) This is incorrect. With the word *yet*, we need an auxiliary verb (*haven't*) and past participle. However, we need to change *spoke* to *spoken* because *spoken* is the past participle.

5. The waiters clean the tables at the end of the day.

a) This is correct. It has a main verb (*clean*).

b) This is incorrect. We need an auxiliary verb (*have*) and a past participle (*cleaned*).

c) This is incorrect. With the subject *waiters*, the main verb should be *cleans*.

6. She has already wrote her pen pal 18 letters.

a) This is correct. With the word *already*, we need an auxiliary verb (*has*) and a main verb (*wrote*).

b) This is incorrect. With the subject *she* and time expression *already*, we need an auxiliary (*has*) and a main verb (*writes*).

c) This is incorrect. *Wrote* is the past tense. With the auxiliary *has*, we need the past participle (*written*).

1 Jack	1 chores	2 suburb
3 apartment	4 vacation	5 medicine

1. _____

2. _____

3. _____

4. _____

5. _____

Exercise 9: ___1) Write a paragraph with 5 sentences or more about one of the topics.
___2) Circle the verbs in your paragraph.

Topic Choices: ___1) Write about a problem that you had when you were younger.
___2) Write about a problem that someone else (for example, your brother, friend, or neighbor) had when he or she was younger.

Unit 19: These, Those, This, That

THE PROBLEMS

These was too old.
This socks has a hole.

Exercise 1: Circle the correct underlined word.

1. This (is)/are   2. These is/are   3. That feels/feel
4. That boy/boys   5. This toy is/are   6. Those men is/are
7. These shoe/shoes   8. Those seems/seem

Exercise 2: Fill in the blanks for the rules with *singular* or *plural*.

1. _____ means only one. The word *boy* is _____.
2. With _____ nouns, we use *this* and *that*.
3. _____ means more than one. The word *boys* is _____.
4. With _____ nouns, we use *these* and *those*.
5. *Is, was, has, goes, needs, wants* go with _____ nouns.
6. *Are, were, have, go, need, want* go with _____ nouns.

Exercise 3: Choose the sentence that is correct in each pair.

1. a) This problem was easy to solve.

   b) This problems was easy to solve.

2. a) The dentist needs to pull these teeth.

   b) The dentist needs to pull this teeth.

3. a) You can eat these apples, but those has bad spots.

   b) You can eat these apples, but those have bad spots.

4. a) He had two reasons for quitting. That was because of money and family.

   b) He had two reasons for quitting. Those were because of money and family.

---

1. _____ computers just crashed.

   a) In the blank, we should write *That* because *computers* is singular.

   b) We should write *Those* because *computers* is plural.

2. I got a good score on my test. That _____ I will pass my class.

   a) We should write *mean* because *That* is singular.

   b) We should write *means* because *That* is singular.

3. Sara has a great job. That job _____ at 10 a.m.

   a) We should write *start* because *job* is singular.

   b) We should write *starts* because *job* is singular.

4. Your car needs new tires, and you should change the oil. _____ _____ the only problems that I found.

   a) We should write *That is* because there is only one problem.

   b) We should write *Those are* because there are two problems.

5. Ken decided to attend a community college before going to a university. This _____ will save him money.

   a) We should write *plan* because *This* is singular.

   b) We should write *plans* because *This* is singular.

6. Three cities wanted to have the Olympics. _____ cities were New York, Paris, and London.

   a) We should write *That* because the word *cities* is singular.

   b) We should write *Those* because the word *cities* is plural.

1. Mimi has a lot of work. This _____ takes her about ten hours to finish.

 a) jobs   b) job

Reason: *We should write the singular noun "job" because of "This."*

2. There are two types of chairs here. These _____ more comfortable than those.

 a) feels   b) feel

Reason: _____

_____

3. I hope you liked the pictures that I got for you. Those _____ hard to find.

 a) was   b) were

Reason: _____

_____

4. This babysitter _____ near my house.

 a) live   b) lives

Reason: _____

_____

5. It's snowing. That _____ everyone can stay home today.

 a) mean   b) means

Reason: _____

_____

6. We must sit in the back during the movie. All of those front_____ are taken.

 a) seat   b) seats

Reason: _____

_____

Exercise 6:   Write the sentences that your teacher reads. Use the words in the box.
The number with each word is the sentence number that the word is in.

1 sugar	2 sweeter	3 boss	4 documents

1. _____

2. _____

3. _____

4. _____

Exercise 7:   Write sentences and use one of the words below in each sentence.
Use each word one time. You should write 4 sentences.

this   these   that   those

_____

_____

_____

_____

_____

_____

_____

_____

Unit 20: Grammar Groups Review
Units 16-19

STUDENT A

Directions: These sentences and questions are about the worksheet in the box below. Read your sentences and questions to your partners.

   1. Look at A. Is there a problem with this sentence? Explain.

   4. Look at D. Is the word *have* an auxiliary verb or main verb?

   7. Look at F. Should we change the word *lost* to the words *have lost?*
      Why or why not?

   10. Look at I. Is there a problem with the auxiliary verb? Explain.

Worksheet

A. Because the restaurant was closed, so we ate at home.

B. Since I have a cold. You should stay away from me.

C. I want to sit near the front because I forgot to bring my glasses.

D. We have a meeting at noon today.

E. Ken hasn't seen that movie yet.

F. I lost 10 pounds last year.

G. Tom can't take Ann to the dance because he already asked Sara
to go with him.

H. <u>This/These</u> dishes are still dirty.

I. Those men was looking for jobs.

J. This bag is mine, but that are theirs.

Unit 20: Grammar Groups Review
Units 16-19

Directions: These sentences and questions are about the worksheet in the box below. Read your sentences and questions to your partners.

2. Look at B. Is there a problem with this sentence? Explain.

5. Look at E. Is the word *hasn't* an auxiliary verb or main verb?

8. Look at G. Should we change the words *already asked* to *has already asked*? Why or why not?

11. Look at J. Is there a problem in this sentence? If so, what should we change?

Worksheet

A. Because the restaurant was closed, so we ate at home.

B. You should stay away from me. Since I have a cold.

C. I want to sit near the front because I forgot to bring my glasses.

D. We have a meeting at noon today.

E. Ken hasn't seen that movie yet.

F. I lost 10 pounds last year.

G. Tom can't take Ann to the dance because he already asked Sara to go with him.

H. This/These dishes are still dirty.

I. Those men was looking for jobs.

J. This bag is mine, but that are theirs.

Unit 20: Grammar Groups Review
Units 16-19

Directions: These sentences and questions are about the worksheet in the box below. Read your sentences and questions to your partners.

3. Look at C. Is it all right to put the word *because* in the middle of a sentence?

6. Look at E. Should we change the verb from *hasn't seen* to *didn't see*? Why or why not?

9. Look at H. Look at the underlined words. Circle the correct one.

12. Look at J. If I change *bag* to *bags*, what other changes should I make?

Worksheet

A. Because the restaurant was closed, so we ate at home.

B. You should stay away from me. Since I have a cold.

C. I want to sit near the front because I forgot to bring my glasses.

D. We have a meeting at noon today.

E. Ken hasn't seen that movie yet.

F. I lost 10 pounds last year.

G. Tom can't take Ann to the dance because he already asked Sara to go with him.

H. This/These dishes are still dirty.

I. Those men was looking for jobs.

J. This bag is mine, but that are theirs.

Unit 21: Gerunds

THE PROBLEMS

Run is good exercise.
I finished read that book.

Exercise 1: Circle the nouns. Ignore pronouns such as *he*. (There are 8 nouns, including *candy*.)

1. He likes (candy.)
2. He likes eating.
3. We enjoy music.
4. We enjoy singing.
5. Books are interesting.
6. Reading is interesting.
7. Cigarettes are dangerous.
8. Smoking is dangerous.

Exercise 2: Choose the correct answers.

1. In Exercise 1, the verb-*ing* forms (*eating, singing, reading*, and *smoking*) are

   _____.

   a) nouns   b) verbs   c) prepositions
2. When a verb-*ing* (*eating, singing*, etc.) is a noun, it is called a _____.
   a) participle   b) verb   c) gerund

Exercise 3: ___1) Look at the pairs of sentences below the box.

___2) In Sentence a, in the blank, write a regular noun from the box.

___3) In Sentence b, in the blank, write a gerund from the box.

Regular nouns:	countries	✔his car	voice
	music	school	computer
Gerunds:	shouting	fixing	studying
	✔driving	traveling	playing

1. a) Tom stopped *his car.*

    b) Tom stopped *driving.*

2. a) My hobby is _____.

    b) My hobby is _____ guitar.

3. a) A _____ is hard to fix.

    b) _____ a computer is hard.

4. a) I like foreign _____.

    b) I like _____.

5. a) _____ makes Jim tired.

    b) _____ makes Jim tired.

6. a) His _____ hurts my ears.

    b) His _____ hurts my ears.

Exercise 4: Look at the sentences. Answer the question after each.

1. Fishing is a good hobby.

    Is the word *fishing* a noun or verb? _____

2. My brother is fishing in the river now.

    Is the word *fishing* a noun or verb? _____

3. **Waiting makes me nervous.**

   Is the word *waiting* a noun or verb? _____

4. **We were waiting for our plane for four hours.**

   Is the word *waiting* a noun or verb? _____

5. **Joni saw some rabbits while she was hiking.**

   Is the word *hiking* a noun or verb? _____

6. **Joni enjoyed hiking.**

   Is the word *hiking* a noun or verb? _____

| **Exercise 5:** | ___1) Write the sentences that your teacher reads to you. |
| | ___2) Circle the gerunds in the sentences. |

1.

2.

3.

4.

5.

Exercise 6:	___1) Write 2 sentences that start with a gerund.
	___2) Write 2 sentences about things that you don't like. Use a gerund in each sentence.
	___3) Write 2 sentences about things that you enjoy doing. Use a gerund in each sentence.
	___4) Write 2 sentences about things that you have stopped doing. Use a gerund in each sentence.

Unit 22: Prepositions and Gerunds

THE PROBLEM

He made some money by work hard.

Exercise 1:   Choose the correct answers. To review prepositions, see Unit 12.

1. A gerund is a ____. For example, *running* is a gerund in this sentence:
   Running is fun.
   a) noun   b) verb   c) preposition

2. After a preposition, we put a _____, for example, in this sentence: *On Saturdays, Dan often exercises.*
   a) noun   b) verb   c) preposition

Exercise 2:   ___1) Circle the prepositions.
                  ___2) Underline the noun after each preposition.

1. They usually go (to) school after they finish work.

2. This is a great computer program (for) learning new English words.

3. My boss gave me a vacation for three days.

4. My boss gave me a vacation for working hard.

5. Ann talked to me about studying.

6. By exercising, Rita got stronger.

7. For my birthday, my parents bought me a car.

8. For winning the game, the team received a trophy.

---

1. From eat too much cake, I gained weight.

    a) This is correct. The noun *eat* is after the preposition *from*.

    b) This is incorrect. We need a gerund (*eating*) after the preposition *from*.

2. The neighbors got upset at Ken for playing loud music.

    a) This is correct. The gerund (*playing*) is after the preposition *for*.

    b) This is incorrect. We need *play* after the preposition *for*.

3. Andy was very tired after drive all night to Seattle.

    a) This is correct. The noun *drive* is after the preposition *after*.

    b) This is incorrect. We need a gerund (*driving*) after the preposition *after*.

4. We found the answer by search the Internet.

    a) This is correct. The noun *search* is after the preposition *by*.

    b) This is incorrect. We need a gerund (*searching*) after the preposition *by*.

Exercise 4: ____1) If the sentence is correct, write *OK*. (3 sentences are OK, including the first.)
____2) If the sentence is incorrect, write *Not OK* and explain why.

_OK_ 1. Tran is very good at building bird houses.

_____

Not OK 2. My tutor gave me a dictionary for look up new words.

It needs the gerund "looking" after the preposition "for."

_____ 3. The mother stopped her child from run into the street.

_____

_____ 4. After live in New York, we moved to Los Angeles.

_____

_____ 5. The policeman gave my brother a ticket for speeding.

_____

_____ 6. By eating good food, we can usually stay healthy.

_____

_____ 7. For save a man's life, Ann received a medal.

_____

Exercise 5:   Write the sentences that your teacher reads to you.

1. _____

2. _____

3. _____

4. _____

Excercise 6:   ___1) Choose a preposition and a gerund from the box and, below, write
a sentence for each pair of words. Use each word only once.
___2) You should write 4 sentences.
___3) Circle each preposition and its gerund.

Prepositions:	about	by	from
	✔ after	for	
Gerunds:	working	traveling	studying
	speaking	✔ playing	

1. _Ken usually takes a nap (after playing) basketball._

2. _____

3. _____

4. _____

5. _____

Unit 23: Quantity Words

THE PROBLEMS

Many person got lost.
Every student need a book.

Exercise 1:   Choose words from the box to fill in the blanks below.

toys	classes	actors
video	passengers	friends

1. Some _____ in that movie are famous.

2. I asked many _____ to help me.

3. He put all the _____ in the box.

4. Fortunately, one of the _____on the plane was a doctor.

5. Ken was a lazy student, so he missed a lot of _____ in college.

6. I have already seen every _____ in that store.

Exercise 2:   Choose the correct answers.

1. After the words, *many, some, all of the, one of the, a lot of,* and *every,* we can write a _____.
   a) noun   b) verb   c) preposition

2. In general, after the words, *many, some, all of the, one of the,* and *a lot of,* we can write a _____.
   a) singular noun, for example, *many boy*
   b) plural noun, for example, *many boys*

3. After the word, *every,* we can write a _____.
   a) singular noun, for example, *every boy*
   b) plural noun, for example, *every boys*

---

1. One of the camper got lost in the forest.

   a) This is correct because after *one of*, we use the singular noun *camper*.

   b) This is incorrect. After *one of*, we should use the plural noun *campers*.

2. I can't talk to you now. I have many appointments today.

   a) This is correct because after *many*, we use the plural noun *appointments*.

   b) This is incorrect. After *many*, we should use the singular noun *appointment*.

3. Ms. Brown was unhappy because her children ate all of the snacks.

   a) This is correct because after *all of*, we use the plural noun *snacks*.

   b) This is incorrect. After *all of*, we should use the singular noun *snack*.

4. In my neighborhood, every families has a swimming pool.

   a) This is correct because after *every*, we use the plural noun *families*.

   b) This is incorrect. After *every*, we should use the singular noun *family*.

5. I need to find some people to help us.

   a) This is correct because after *some*, we use the plural noun *people*.

   b) This is incorrect. After *some*, we should use the singular noun *person*.

6. There were a lot of message on my answering machine.

   a) This is correct because after *a lot of*, we use the singular noun *message*.

   b) This is incorrect because after *a lot of*, we should use the plural noun *messages*.

feel	were	sleeps
want	have	is

1. Many patients _____ to see the doctor these days.

2. All of the rooms in my house _____ cold today.

3. It was snowing, so a lot of guests _____ late for the party last night.

4. Some vegetables _____ bad spots on them, so be careful.

5. One of the drivers _____ waving at us.

6. Every child _____ for 30 minutes in the afternoon.

Exercise 5: Choose the correct answers in the box below.

1. After the words *many, some, all of the,* and *a lot of,* we write a _____ .
   a) singular verb, for example, *many is*
   b) plural verb, for example, *many are*
2. After the words *one of the* and *every*, we write a _____ .
   a) singular verb, for example, *one of the cats is* or *every cat is*
   b) plural verb, for example, *one of the cats are* or *every cat are*

1. A lot of homes _____ have air conditioners in our area.

   a) doesn't   b) don't

   Reason: *We should use the plural verb after "a lot of."*

2. There are some _____ in the sky tonight.

   a) cloud   b) clouds

   Reason: *We should use a plural noun after "some."*

3. After the race, all of the _____ felt tired.

   a) runner   b) runners

   Reason: _____

4. One of our _____ is bright red.

   a) tree   b) trees

   Reason: _____

5. Every hotel _____ filled this weekend.

   a) is   b) are

   Reason: _____

6. Many colleges _____ scholarships to outstanding students.

   a) gives   b) give

   Reason: _____

7. Some diseases _____ difficult to cure.

   a) is   b) are

   Reason: _____

8. One of the computers _____ a virus.

   a) has   b) have

   Reason: _____

9. All of the stores _____ at 5 p.m. on Sundays.

   a) closes   b) close

   Reason: _____

10. They gave prizes to every _____ at the party.

   a) child   b) children

   Reason: _____

Exercise 7: Write the sentences that your teacher reads to you.

1. _____

2. _____

3. _____

4. _____

5. _____

Exercise 8: ___1) Write a paragraph with 5 sentences or more about the topic below.
 ___2) In at least 3 sentences, use one of these expressions: *many, some, all of the, a lot of, one of the* or *every.*

Topic: Describe your city and your favorite places in it.

Unit 24: Starting Sentences with Prepositions

THE PROBLEMS

In the city find good jobs.
At the beach is beautiful.

Exercise 1: ___1) Circle the prepositional phrases. Remember from Unit 12, a prepositional phrase is a preposition and a noun after it. (There are 6 prepositional phrases, including the first.)
___2) Write *S* above the subject of each sentence.

                                                    S
1. (Near the mall,) we can find some cheap electronic shops.

2. After an hour, they decided to go home.

3. Under the table, the dog found some food.

4. In the middle of the night, the baby woke up.

5. In the desert, it is very hot.

Exercise 2: Choose the correct answer.

The subject of a sentence _____ part of the prepositional phrase.
   a) can be   b) cannot be

1. **Next to my bed, I have a lamp and some books.**

   a) This is correct. The subject *I* is after the prepositional phrase.

   b) This is incorrect because it doesn't have a subject after the prepositional phrase. We should add *it* after *bed*.

2. **At night is very cold in winter.**

   a) This is correct. The subject *night* is after the prepositional phrase.

   b) This is incorrect because it doesn't have a subject after the prepositional phrase. We should add the word *it* after *night*.

3. **During the game, a player got hurt.**

   a) This is correct. The subject *player* is after the prepositional phrase.

   b) This is incorrect because it doesn't have a subject after the prepositional phrase.

4. **In my city is a lot of traffic during the rush hour.**

   a) This is correct. The subject *city* is after the prepositional phrase.

   b) This is incorrect because it doesn't have a subject after the prepositional phrase. We should add *there* after *city*.

Exercise 4:   ___1) If a sentence is correct, write *OK*. (2 sentences are OK, including Sentence 2.)
           ___2) If a sentence is incorrect, write *Not OK* and explain why.

Not OK 1. **Next to the library found a beautiful park with a lot of trees.**

It needs a subject after the prepositional phrase.

*OK*____ 2. **At the party, everyone had a great time.**

_____ 3. **For an hour did my homework for English class.**

_____ 4. **On a cell phone called 911 to report the accident.**

_____ 5. From the policeman, my brother got a ticket for speeding.

_____

_____ 6. Inside the theater watched a movie and ate pop corn.

_____

Exercise 5: ___1) Write the sentences that your teacher reads to you.
___2) Circle the subject in each sentence.

1. _____
2. _____
3. _____
4. _____
5. _____

Exercise 6: Write 4 sentences. Start each sentence with a preposition. You can use the prepositions in the box.

in	at	near	on	from
by	for	next to	during	under

1. _____
2. _____
3. _____
4. _____

Unit 25: Grammar Groups Review
Units 21-24

Directions: These sentences and questions are about the worksheet in the box below. Read your sentences and questions to your partners.

1. Look at A. Is there a problem with this sentence?

4. Look at D. Is there a problem with the word *ride*? Explain.

7. In G, write a sentence starting with a gerund. Circle the gerund.

10. Look at I. Should we change the word *make* to *makes*? Why or why not?

Worksheet

A. At the doctor's office can get some medicine for the flu.

B. Sending letters is more expensive than using email.

C. My father is helping me fix my old car.

D. Ann enjoys ride horses.

E. Yesterday, my teacher stopped me from made a mistake.

F. After finishing this class, we should go to a coffee shop.

G. _____

H. _____

I. A lot of movie make me laugh.

J. One of the cookie/cookies is/are for my friend.

K. Sara brought all of her photo/photos to the party.

Unit 25: Grammar Groups Review
Units 21-24

Directions: These sentences and questions are about the worksheet in the box below. Read your sentences and questions to your partners.

2. Look at B. Is the word *sending* a gerund?

5. Look at E. Should we change the word *made* to *make* or *making*?
   Why or why not?

8. In H, write a sentence starting with a preposition and gerund.

11. Look at J. Look at the underlined words. Circle the correct ones.

Worksheet

A. At the doctor's office can get some medicine for the flu.

B. Sending letters is more expensive than using email.

C. My father is helping me fix my old car.

D. Ann enjoys ride horses.

E. Yesterday, my teacher stopped me from made a mistake.

F. After finishing this class, we should go to a coffee shop.

G. _____

H. _____

I. A lot of movie make me laugh.

J. One of the cookie/cookies is/are for my friend.

K. Sara brought all of her photo/photos to the party.

Unit 25: Grammar Groups Review
Units 21-24

Directions: These sentences and questions are about the worksheet in the box below. Read your sentences and questions to your partners.

3. Look at C. Is the word *helping* a gerund?

6. Look at F. Is there a problem with the words *after finishing*? Explain.

9. Look at I. Should we change the word *movie* to *movies*? Why or why not?

12. Look at K. Look at the underlined words. Circle the correct one.

Worksheet

A. At the doctor's office can get some medicine for the flu.

B. Sending letters is more expensive than using email.

C. My father is helping me fix my old car.

D. Ann enjoys ride horses.

E. Yesterday, my teacher stopped me from made a mistake.

F. After finishing this class, we should go to a coffee shop.

G. _____

H. _____

I. A lot of movie make me laugh.

J. One of the cookie/cookies is/are for my friend.

K. Sara brought all of her photo/photos to the party.

Unit 26: Semi-Auxiliary Verbs
be able to/be supposed to/
be going to/have to

THE PROBLEMS

We able to write the report.
Ann is supposed finishing soon.

Exercise 1:   Choose words from the box to fill in the blanks below.

fix	take	pay	leave

1. We are supposed to _____ our rent today.

2. The workers were able to _____ the problem with the electricity.

3. Camille is going to _____ for California soon.

4. Miyuki can't help her mother because she has to _____ her dog for a walk.

Exercise 2:   Choose the correct answers.

1. After semi-auxiliary BE + *able to, supposed to, going to*, and HAVE + *to*, we use____.
   a) the base form of the verb
   b) the *-ing* form of the verb
   c) the past form of the verb
2. BE + *able to, supposed to, going to*, and HAVE+ *to* are called _____.
   a) subjects
   b) semi-auxiliary verbs

Exercise 3: ___1) Choose the correct sentence in each pair.
___2) In each correct sentence, underline the semi-auxiliary verb and circle the base form of the verb.

1. a) They supposed to visit their relatives during the holidays.
   (b) They <u>are supposed to</u> (visit) their relatives during the holidays.
2. a) We were able to see some wild animals in the forest.
   b) We were able to saw some wild animals in the forest.
3. a) Ken going to bring a dessert to the potluck dinner.
   b) Ken is going to bring a dessert to the potluck dinner.
4. a) Travelers have to arrive at the airport early.
   b) Travelers have to arriving at the airport early.
5. a) My boss became angry because I was supposed to finishing the project two days ago.
   b) My boss became angry because I was supposed to finish the project two days ago.
6. a) Ravi able to fly the plane safely during the storm.
   b) Ravi was able to fly the plane safely during the storm.

Exercise 4: Correct the mistakes with semi-auxiliary verbs and main verbs. (There are 5, including *to*.)

[1.] These days, airline tickets are becoming more expensive. [2.] However, it is possible to find cheap ones. [3.] Some people are able ^to^ find cheap tickets by flying on new airlines. [4.] You going to get the best price if you fly on Tuesdays, Wednesdays, and Saturdays. [5.] Early morning flights are cheap, but you usually have to making at least one stop. [6.] A good idea is to reserve 21 days in advance. [7.] For holidays, we supposed to buy our tickets even earlier. [8.] Finally, sometimes, we can able to get a discount from the airlines if we also buy a package with a rental car.

Exercise 5:   Write the sentences that your teacher reads to you.

1.

2.

3.

4.

Exercise 6:   Write at least 4 sentences about each of these topics:
____1) what you're able to do right now.
____2) what you're going to do tomorrow.
____3) what you have to do next week.
____4) what people are supposed to eat in order to stay healthy.

Unit 27: Although

THE PROBLEMS

Although I was late.
Although I'm hungry, but I won't eat anything.

Exercise 1: Circle the clauses. Remember from Unit 11, a clause has a subject and a verb. (There are 10 clauses, including the 2 in Sentence 1.)

1. (Ken is wearing shorts today) although (the weather is cold.)

2. Ellen went to a party although her parents told her to stay home.

3. Although guns are dangerous, some people have them.

4. Children sometimes don't like to eat vegetables although they are good for our health.

5. Although the class was canceled, some students came anyway.

Exercise 2: Choose the correct answer.

When we use *although* in a sentence, we have ___.
    a) one clause   b) two clauses

Exercise 3: Choose the correct sentence in each pair.

1. a) Although Jim is tired, but he will continue to play.
   b) Although Jim is tired, ~~but~~ he will continue to play.

2. a) Although Gina loves snow, but she doesn't like to ski.
   b) Although Gina loves snow, ~~but~~ she doesn't like to ski.

When we use *Although* at the start of a sentence, we _____ the word *but* in the sentence.

a) use   b) do not use

Exercise 5: Look at the sentences. Choose the correct explanation for each.

1. Although Tom is 18 years old, he doesn't have his driver's license.

   a) This sentence is correct because it has two clauses, and one of them begins with *although*.

   b) This sentence is incorrect because it has only one clause with *although*.

2. Although steak is expensive, but we eat it every weekend.

   a) This sentence is correct because it has two clauses, and one of them begins with *although*.

   b) This sentence is incorrect because it has *although* and *but*.

3. Although Ann loves goldfish.

   a) This sentence is correct because it has two clauses and one of them begins with *although*.

   b) This sentence is incorrect because it has only one clause with *although*.

4. Tom refused to go to the dentist. Although he had a toothache.

   a) These sentences are correct because they are two clauses and one of them begins with *although*.

   b) The first sentence is correct, but the second one is incorrect because it has only one clause and it begins with *although*.

5. Although my car has only 18,000 miles, but it needs new tires.

   a) This sentence is correct because it has two clauses, and one of them begins with *although*.

   b) This sentence is incorrect because it has *although* and *but*.

6. I love to paint pictures although I'm not very good at it.

   a) This sentence is correct because it has two clauses, and one of them begins with *although*.

   b) This sentence is incorrect because it has only one clause with *although*.

Exercise 6: ___1) If the sentence is correct, write *OK*. (2 are OK, including
Sentence 2).
___2) If the sentence is incorrect, write *Not OK* and explain why.

Not OK 1. Although she lives in a large house.

_____ *It needs a second clause.* _____

_OK_ 2. Sam doesn't play basketball although he is very tall.

_____ 3. Although they plan to get married, but they haven't chosen a date yet.

_____ 4. There are wars in many places these days although everyone
wants peace.

_____ 5. Toni's family likes Asian food. Although they don't know how
to use chopsticks.

Exercise 7: Write the sentences that your teacher reads to you.

1.

2.

3.

4.

5.

Exercise 8: ___1) Write a paragraph with 5 sentences or more about one of the topics below.

___2) In at least 2 of the sentences, use the word *although*.

Topic Choices: ___1) Write about a time when you were nervous.

___2) Write about a time when you worked very hard, but you were not successful.

Unit 28: Adjective Clauses with Who

THE PROBLEMS

The man who is sitting there.
The woman lives near my house is nice.
I talked to the girl who she is my roommate.

Exercise 1: Circle the *who* clauses. Remember from Unit 11, a clause has a subject and verb. (There are 4 *who* clauses, including the clause in Sentence 1).

1. I helped a boy (who is a student at this college.)

2. A dentist who drives a Mercedes lives on the corner.

3. During the holiday, we often give money to people who need help.

4. The girl who found the lost dog got a reward from the owner.

Exercise 2: ____1) Circle the *who* clauses (in other words, the dependent clauses).
____2) Write *S* above the subject of the main clauses (independent clauses).
____3) Write *V* above the verb of the main clauses.
____4) Write a small *s* above the subject of the *who* clauses (dependent clauses).
____5) Write a small *v* above the verb of the *who* clauses.

    S   V   s   v

1. Tom went to the game with some friends (who had free tickets.)

    S s   v   V

2. A man (who has a good voice) works in a radio station.

3. The woman always helps people who have trouble.

4. Mari translates for her relatives who don't speak English.

5. Mothers who work outside their homes are often very busy.

6. A professor who lives in Seattle won an award.

Unit 28: Adjective Clauses with Who • 113

When we use the word *who* in a sentence, we should have _____ .
a) one clause   b) two clauses

Exercise 4:   Look at the sentences. Choose the correct explanation for each.

1. The man who is standing over there.

   a) This sentence is correct because it has two clauses and one of them has *who*.
   b) This sentence is incorrect because it has only one clause with *who*.

2. A woman who graduated from college last year and found a job at a travel agency in New York.

   a) This sentence is correct because it has two clauses and one of them has *who*.
   b) This sentence is incorrect because there is no verb for the subject *the woman*.

3. The bus driver who drives my bus plays chess in his free time.

   a) This sentence is correct because it has two clauses and one of them has *who*.
   b) This sentence is incorrect because there is no verb for the subject *driver*.

4. I get angry at people who cut in line at a movie theater.

   a) This sentence is correct because it has two clauses and one of them has *who*.
   b) This sentence is incorrect because it has only one clause with *who*.

5. My neighbor works in an office wears a suit to work every day.

   a) This sentence is correct because there is only one clause.
   b) This sentence is incorrect because we need to add the word *who* after *neighbor*.

6. Ann loves to work with children who under five years old.

   a) This sentence is correct because it has two clauses and one of them has *who*.
   b) This sentence is incorrect because there is no verb in the *who* clause.

7. The store manager interviewed three people who they wanted the job.

   a) This sentence is correct because it has two clauses and one of them has *who*.
   b) This sentence is incorrect because there are two subjects in the *who* clause (*who* and *they*).

Exercise 5: Look at the sentences.
  ___1) If the sentence is correct, write *OK*. (2 sentences are OK, including the first.)
  ___2) If the sentence is incorrect, write *Not OK* and explain why.

_OK_____ 1. The girl who is playing the guitar is very talented.

Not OK 2. The basketball player who is seven feet tall.
_____*We need a verb for the subject "player."*_____

_____ 3. Only people who bought a ticket can go.

_____ 4. The woman who in the car looks like my teacher.

_____ 5. The pilot is flying our plane comes from my city.

_____ 6. The actor who he won the award plans to make an action movie next year.

_____ 7. The man who was driving his car too fast.

_____ 8. The students pass their final exams will graduate.

Exercise 6: Correct the mistakes in the paragraph. (There are 4 mistakes.)

[1.] I just returned from a great trip overseas. [2.] I went on the trip with some friends who were my roommates in college. [3.] We spent three weeks in Europe. [4.] One of my friends who he spoke French became our tour guide in Paris. [5.] His name was Tony. [6.] Tony introduced us to an artist was famous. [7.] The artist showed us some of his pictures. ^{8.} I bought one of them for my sister who an artist, too. ^{9.} Also, my other traveling friend who spoke German. ^{10.} He translated for us in Germany.

Exercise 7: Write the sentences that your teacher reads to you.

1.

2.

3.

4.

5.

Exercise 8: ___1) Write a paragraph with 5 sentences or more about one of the topics below.
___2) In at least 2 of the sentences, use the word *who* in a clause.

Topic Choices: ___1) Write about your teachers from your elementary or high school.

___2) Write about your friends from your elementary or high school.

Unit 29: Subject + Prepositional Phrase + Verb

THE PROBLEMS

The man in front of you he is my teacher.
Flowers in the sun needs a lot of water.

Exercise 1: ____1) Circle the prepositions. (There are 8 prepositions, including those in Sentences 1 and 2).
____2) Underline the noun after each preposition.

---

1. He went (to) his <u>office</u> after he had eaten breakfast.

2. They played basketball (in) the <u>gym</u> (for) three <u>hours</u>.

3. You will find your seat in the first-class section of the airplane.

4. He went to the zoo by himself.

5. For lunch, I made a sandwich.

Exercise 2: ____1) Write *S* above the subjects.
____2) Write *V* above the verbs.
____3) Circle the prepositions.
____4) Underline the noun after each preposition.

      S   V

1. The girl (in) the blue <u>dress</u> knows the answers.

2. The tree in Jim's front yard has a large nest near the top.

3. The big house on the corner looks scary.

4. The old man with the cane wants your help.

5. The spaghetti on the stove is for our dinner.

6. The doctor in the emergency area at the hospital gave medicine to the patient.

---

1. The boy in the front row he has a question.

   a) This is a correct sentence.

   b) This is incorrect. The subject is *boy*, so we don't need *he*.

2. The old car under the trees has a flat tire.

   a) This is a correct sentence.

   b) This is incorrect. We need to add a subject before *has*.

3. Most flowers in Dan's yard gets a lot of sun.

   a) This is a correct sentence.

   b) This is incorrect. The subject is *flowers*, so the verb should be *get*.

4. The bus with the red top goes to the university.

   a) This is a correct sentence.

   b) This is incorrect. There is no verb.

5. The envelope on the corner of the desk for my friend.

   a) This is a correct sentence.

   b) This is incorrect. There is no verb.

1. a) The umbrella near the windows belongs to Ben.

   b) The umbrella near the windows belong to Ben.

2. a) The insects in my garden bad this year.

   b) The insects in my garden are bad this year.

3. a) The apartments with a view of the ocean they are the most expensive.

   b) The apartments with a view of the ocean are the most expensive.

4. a) The man in the back of the room near the magazines is leaving soon.

   b) The man in the back of the room near the magazines are leaving soon.

| Exercise 5: | ___1) Write the sentences that your teacher reads to you. |
| | ___2) Write *S* above the subjects and *V* above the verbs. |

1.

2.

3.

4.

5.

| Exercise 6: | Write 4 sentences. In each, write a subject + prepositional phrase + verb. (See Exercise 2 for examples.) |

Unit 30: Grammar Groups Review
Units 26-29

Directions: These sentences and questions are about the worksheet in the box below. Read your sentences and questions to your partners.

1. Look at A. Is there a problem with this sentence? Explain.
4. Look at C. How can we correct this sentence?
7. Look at F. Write *S* above the subject.
10. Look at H. Is there a problem with the underlined words? Explain.

Worksheet

A. Although it was Patti's birthday, but nobody gave her a present.

B. Marie still smokes cigarettes. Although she tried to quit often.

C. The nurse who helped my grandmother.

D. The little boy is sitting on the bench is looking for his mother.

E. My parents gave a tip to the waiter who he served them dinner.

F. The flowers in the blue pot <u>needs/need</u> some water.

G. The cars at the back of the parking lot they are expensive.

H. When you read, <u>you supposed to use</u> a good light.

I. Last week, I was able to <u>find/found</u> an Internet site for my report.

J. She <u>going to</u> leave early for work.

Unit 30: Grammar Groups Review
Units 26-29

Directions: These sentences and questions are about the worksheet in the box below. Read your sentences and questions to your partners.

    2. Look at B. Is there a problem with this sentence? Explain.

    5. Look at D. Where should we add the word *who* ?

    8. Look at F. Which underlined verb is correct? Explain.

    11. Look at I. Which underlined word is correct? Explain.

Worksheet

A. Although it was Patti's birthday, but nobody gave her a present.

B. Marie still smokes cigarettes. Although she tried to quit often.

C. The nurse who helped my grandmother.

D. The little boy is sitting on the bench is looking for his mother.

E. My parents gave a tip to the waiter who he served them dinner.

F. The flowers in the blue pot <u>needs/need</u> some water.

G. The cars at the back of the parking lot they are expensive.

H. When you read, <u>you supposed to use</u> a good light.

I. Last week, I was able to <u>find/found</u> an Internet site for my report.

J. She <u>going to</u> leave early for work.

Unit 30: Grammar Groups Review
Units 26-29

Directions: These sentences and questions are about the worksheet in the box below. Read your sentences and questions to your partners.

3. Look at C. Write an *S* above the subject and *V* above the verb.

6. Look at E. Correct the mistake.

9. Look at G. Is there a problem with this sentence?

12. Look at J. Look at the underlined words. Is there a problem?

Worksheet

A. Although it was Patti's birthday, but nobody gave her a present.

B. Marie still smokes cigarettes. Although she tried to quit often.

C. The nurse who helped my grandmother.

D. The little boy is sitting on the bench is looking for his mother.

E. My parents gave a tip to the waiter who he served them dinner.

F. The flowers in the blue pot <u>needs / need</u> some water.

G. The cars at the back of the parking lot they are expensive.

H. When you read, <u>you supposed to use</u> a good light.

I. Last week, I was able to <u>find / found</u> an Internet site for my report.

J. She <u>going to</u> leave early for work.

Unit 31: Possessives

THE PROBLEMS

I don't like my photo, but I love your's.
My car has a problem. It's tires are flat.

Exercise 1:   ___1) Fill in the blanks below with words from the box.
                   ___2) Circle the word after each blank.

her	his	my	your
	their	its	our

1. Jason showed me _____ (stereo) yesterday.

2. After you finish writing it, you should take _____ letter to the post office.

3. _____ house is beautiful, but they think that it is too small.

4. Diane found _____ glasses under some magazines.

5. My brother and I discussed _____ plans for four hours.

6. I bought a new collar for _____ dog.

7. Maria likes her computer because _____ screen is very clear.

Exercise 2:   Choose the correct answer.

In Exercise 1 above, I circled _____.
   a) verbs   b) nouns   c) prepositions

___1) If the underlined word is correct, write *OK*. (3 are OK, including the first.)
___2) If the underlined word is incorrect, write *Wrong*. Then correct the mistake.

_OK_   1. I like to secretly listen to <u>their</u> conversation.

                                              her

Wrong 2. Ann gave money to ~~hers~~ ^ children for lunch.

_____ 3. If you need to make a call, you can use <u>my</u> cellphone.

_____ 4. Did you get answers to <u>yours</u> questions?

_____ 5. Mimi loves that bird. <u>It's</u> song is beautiful.

_____ 6. I always forget <u>her's</u> name.

_____ 7. <u>Our</u> neighbor is moving soon.

Exercise 4: ___1) Fill in the blanks below with words from the box.
___2) Circle the word after each blank.

children's	car's	Tim's	men's
Sara's	boys'	boy's	

1. Did you hear _____ speech about his experiment?

2. I didn't like that _____ engine, so I didn't buy it.

3. There is one other boy in the club. That _____ parents are coming to the party.

4. There are many boys in the club. Those _____ parents are coming to the party.

5. _____ sister looks exactly like her.

6. We're looking for the _____ department.

7. There are a lot of toys in the _____ room.

Exercise 5: Choose the correct answer.

In Exercise 4 above, I circled _____.
a) nouns   b) verbs   c) prepositions

Exercise 6: ___1) If the underlined word is correct, write *OK*. (2 are OK.)
___2) If the underlined word is incorrect, write *Wrong*, and correct the mistake.

Wrong   1. The doctor said that *Steve's* ~~Steves~~ health is great.

_____ 2. I need to get that <u>girl's</u> email address.

_____ 3. Ken was surprised at that <u>books'</u> price.

_____ 4. Five travelers wanted to go to Europe. However, those <u>traveler's</u> passports expired.

_____ 5. <u>Jan's</u> cell phone has an interesting ring.

Exercise 7: Choose the correct answers.

1. *The boy's book, the car's color, the building's steps*: These expressions mean that there _____ boy, car, and building.
   a) is only one   b) are more than one

2. *The boys' books, the cars' color, the buildings' steps*: These expressions mean that there _____ boy, car, and building.
   a) is only one   b) are more than one

Exercise 8: ___1) Fill in the blanks below with words from the box.
___2) If there is a word after the blank, circle it.

theirs	yours	mine
his	ours	hers

1. Tom took his water bottle, but I left _____ at home.

2. I have Jim's and Patti's desserts. Is this one his dessert, or is it _____?

3. I like my new T-shirt, but if you don't like _____ , of course, you can return it.

4. Lisa made lunch for herself and her parents. Then she put her lunch in a bag, and she put _____ in a box.

5. Brad has a red car, and we have a blue car. Brad doesn't like _____, but we really like _____ .

Exercise 9: Choose the correct answer.

In Exercise 8 above, what types of words came after the blanks?
a) nouns   b) not nouns

Exercise 10: Look at the sentences. Choose the correct explanation for each.

1. You should show your pictures to a magazine editor.

   a) This is correct. After *your*, we have a noun.
   b) This is incorrect. In front of a noun, we should write *yours*.

2. Tad visited hers house, but nobody was at home.

   a) This is correct. After *hers*, we have a noun.
   b) This is incorrect. In front of a noun, we should write *her*.

3. That gray horse is walking slowly. I think it hurt it's leg.

   a) This is correct. After *it's,* we have a noun.
   b) This is incorrect. In front of a noun, we should write *its*.

4. The forest was beautiful. All the trees' leaves were yellow and red.

   a) This is correct. We write *trees'* because there is more than one tree, and there is a noun (*leaves*) after it.

   b) This is incorrect. We should write *tree's* because there is more than one tree, and there is a noun (*leaves*) after it.

5. Judy's job was very hard, so she quit.

   a) This is correct. After *Judy's*, we have a noun.

   b) This is incorrect. In front of a noun, we should write *Judys*.

6. Can I borrow your umbrella? I can't find mine umbrella.

   a) This is correct. After *mine*, we have a noun.

   b) This is incorrect. After *mine*, we should not have a noun.

7. Sam and Tami usually visit their's grandchildren during the holidays.

   a) This is correct. After *their's*, we have a noun.

   b) This is incorrect. In front of a noun, we should write *their*. Also, *their's* is not a word.

8. The waiter served dinner to the other people, but he forgot our's.

   a) This is correct. After *our's*, we do not have a noun.

   b) This is incorrect. We should write *ours* because it is not followed by a noun. Also, *our's* is not a word.

Exercise 11: Correct the mistakes with possessives. (There are 6, including *his*.)

¹· Joey is careful about how he spends ^*his* money. ²· Before he buys something, he takes a lot of time to think about it. ³· One time, he wanted to buy a computer, but he didn't buy it because it's keyboard was strange. ⁴· I showed him mine, but he didn't like it either. ⁵· I told him that all computer's keyboards are similar. ⁶· He didn't agree. ⁷· Another time, he wanted to buy a present for

his girlfriend, Ann. [8.] He knew her electric blankets' controls were broken, so he wanted to buy a new one. [9.] Anns electric blanket was soft. [10.] Joey wanted to get another one like her's. [11.] It took him a week to find one.

Exercise 12:	Write the sentences that your teacher reads to you.

1.

2.

3.

4.

5.

Exercise 13:	___1)	Write a paragraph with 5 sentences or more about one of the topics below.
	___2)	In at least 3 of the sentences, use a possessive word.

Topic Choices: ___1) Describe some things that your family members own.
            ___2) Compare your home and your friend's home.

Unit 32: Run-on Sentences

THE PROBLEM

We went to the movies they stayed home.

Exercise 1: ___1) Circle the clauses. (There are 16 clauses, including the 4 in Sentence 1.)

___2) Circle the letter of the correct sentence in each pair.

1.
a) (I like ballet.) (She prefers sports.)
    S V   S   V

b) (I like ballet) (she prefers sports)
    S V   S   V

2.
    S   V   S AV   V
a) The mail came on Monday it didn't come on Tuesday.

    S   V   S AV   V
b) The mail came on Monday. It didn't come on Tuesday.

3.
    S V   S   V
a) Ken ate dinner he finished his homework.

    S V   S   V
b) Ken ate dinner. He finished his homework.

4.
    S V   S   V
a) Ann needs some help. Her children are sick.

    S V   S   V
b) Ann needs some help her children are sick.

Exercise 2: Choose the correct answer.

The incorrect sentences in Exercise 1 are called _____.

a) prepositional phrases   b) run-on sentences   c) fragments

Exercise 3: ___1) Write *S* and *V* above the subjects and verbs.
___2) If a sentence is correct, write *OK*.
___3) If it is a run-on sentence, write *RO*.

$$S \quad V \qquad\qquad S \quad V$$

_OK_ 1. Chen talked to his teacher. She helped him with the assignment.

$$S \quad V \qquad\qquad\qquad S \quad V$$

_RO_ 2. She gave money to her kids for lunch they spent it on candy.

_____ 3. We watched TV they read their books.

_____ 4. Jan decided to go home her husband wanted to stay.

_____ 5. Ken wanted to see a comedy. His friends preferred an action movie.

_____ 6. Our team won the game we celebrated all night.

_____ 7. I forgot to pay the cashier. He looked upset.

1. a) Jack paid the rent he didn't pay the electric bill.
   b) Jack paid the rent, but he didn't pay the electric bill.
   c) Jack paid the rent. He didn't pay the electric bill.
2. a) Tina brought flowers to the party. Bob brought a cake.
   b) Tina brought flowers to the party, and Bob brought a cake.
   c) Tina brought flowers to the party Bob brought a cake.
3. a) The park was closed, so we went to the beach.
   b) The park was closed we went to the beach.
   c) The park was closed. We went to the beach.
4. a) I finished my dinner. I was still hungry.
   b) I finished my dinner I was still hungry.
   c) I finished my dinner, but I was still hungry.

1. We spent the day flying kites, so we are tired now.

   a) This is correct. There are two clauses, and they are connected with comma + *so*.

   b) This is a run-on. There are two clauses. We need a period after *kites*.

2. Her shoes were old she threw them away.

   a) This is correct. There is one clause.

   b) This is a run-on. We could add a period after *old* and capitalize *She*.

3. Ken cut his finger with a very sharp knife during dinner.

   a) This is correct. There is one clause.

   b) This is a run-on. There are two clauses. We can add a period after *finger* and capitalize *with*.

4. It was very cold the children played outside.

   a) This is correct. There is one clause.

   b) This is a run-on. There are two clauses. After *cold*, we could add comma + *but*.

Exercise 6 :   ____1) Write *OK* if the sentence is correct. (2 sentences are OK.)
   ____2) Write *RO* if it is a run-on sentence and explain the mistake.

RO 1. They won their match they were very excited.

Explanation: *We should put a period after "match" and capitalize "They."*

____ 2. I love warm summer nights with cool breezes.

Explanation: _____

____ 3. The newspaper had my picture in it, so I got ten copies.

Explanation: _____

____ 4. Dan's back was hurting he stayed home from work.

Explanation: _____

____ 5. The coffee was cold we didn't drink any.

Explanation: _____

Correct the mistakes with run-on sentences. (There are 4 mistakes, including *but*.)

1. Ted's alarm rang at 6:30. 2. Unfortunately, he planned to wake up at 6 a.m. 3. He wanted to sleep an extra 10 minutes, ^*but* he couldn't because he was already late. 4. He jumped out of bed he got dressed in a hurry. 5. In the kitchen, he quickly drank some coffee, but he didn't eat breakfast. 6. He was able to catch the 7:15 bus he was still late for his meeting at 8 a.m. 7. At 8:15, the bus arrived in front of his office. 8. He walked into the meeting room at 8:25 his boss looked upset.

Exercise 8: Write the sentences that your teacher reads to you.

1.

2.

3.

4.

5.

Exercise 9: Write 6 sentences according to the instructions.

1) Write 2 run-on sentences:

_____

_____

2) Write 2 sentences with 2 clauses with *and, but,* or *so* between them:

_____

_____

3) Write 2 sentences with 2 clauses in each with a period between them:

_____

_____

Unit 33: Grammar Groups Review
Units 31-32

Directions: These sentences and questions are about the worksheet in the box below. Read your sentences and questions to your partners.

1. In A, is there a mistake with the word *her's*? Explain.

4. In D, in the second sentence, is there a mistake with the word *students'*? Explain.

7. Look at G. Draw circles around the clauses.

10. Look at H. Draw circles around the clauses.

13. Look at I. Is this a run-on sentence?

Worksheet

A. Ann likes to feed steak to her's dogs.

B. I found my coat, but Sara didn't find hers.

C. Tomoko bought a new car. It's/Its color is blue.

D. There are 18 students in our class. It takes the teacher five hours to read all the students' essays.

E. We brought our reports, but they forgot their's.

F. You are sitting in mine chair.

G. Someone stole Tom's wallet he called the police.

H. I was supposed to call you, but I didn't have a cell phone.

I. Sasha showed me her office it has a beautiful view

Unit 33: Grammar Groups Review
Units 31-32

Directions: These sentences and questions are about the worksheet in the box below. Read your sentences and questions to your partners.

2. In B, is there a mistake with the word *hers*? Explain.

5. In E, is there a mistake with the word *their's*? Explain.

8. Look at G. Is this a run-on sentence?

11. Look at H. Underline the conjunction.

14. Look at I. Where should we add capitals and periods?

Worksheet

A. Ann likes to feed steak to her's dogs.

B. I found my coat, but Sara didn't find hers.

C. Tomoko bought a new car. It's/Its color is blue.

D. There are 18 students in our class. It takes the teacher five hours to read all the students' essays.

E. We brought our reports, but they forgot their's.

F. You are sitting in mine chair.

G. Someone stole Tom's wallet he called the police.

H. I was supposed to call you, but I didn't have a cell phone.

I. Sasha showed me her office it has a beautiful view

Unit 33: Grammar Groups Review
Units 31-32

Directions: These sentences and questions are about the worksheet in the box below. Read your sentences and questions to your partners.

3. In C, which underlined word is correct?

6. In F, explain why we shouldn't use the word *mine*.

9. Look at G. How can we correct this mistake?

12. Look at H. Is this a run-on sentence? Explain.

Worksheet

A. Ann likes to feed steak to her's dogs.

B. I found my coat, but Sara didn't find hers.

C. Tomoko bought a new car. <u>It's/Its</u> color is blue.

D. There are 18 students in our class. It takes the teacher five hours to read all the students' essays.

E. We brought our reports, but they forgot their's.

F. You are sitting in mine chair.

G. Someone stole Tom's wallet he called the police.

H. I was supposed to call you, but I didn't have a cell phone.

I. Sasha showed me her office it has a beautiful view

Scripts for Listening Exercises

In Units 1-9, the underlined words are the words that are missing in the students' exercise pages.

Unit 1

1. Ann <u>bought</u> a new <u>TV</u>.
2. Some <u>people</u> are afraid of <u>dogs</u>.
3. A <u>policeman gave</u> Ken a <u>ticket</u>.
4. My <u>classmates</u> made <u>presents</u> for <u>our teacher</u>.

Unit 2

1. <u>I have</u> a new CD player.
2. <u>They drank</u> a lot of <u>water</u>.
3. She <u>is</u> happy <u>to live</u> here.
4. My <u>sister got</u> a pet for her <u>birthday</u>.
5. <u>The doctor gave</u> me some medicine.

Unit 3

1. <u>Mary</u> showed us a great <u>web site</u>.
2. <u>His uncle</u> is the president of a company.
3. The newspaper <u>has</u> a picture of <u>me</u> in it.
4. <u>The mailman</u> came to my <u>house</u> around noon.

Unit 4

1. <u>My hobby</u> is bird-watching.
2. <u>Her grandfather</u> retired last year.
3. Carlos <u>lives</u> in an <u>expensive</u> condo.
4. We <u>like</u> the four seasons <u>in our</u> part of Canada.
5. Ann <u>made dinner</u> for everyone <u>in the</u> family.

Unit 6

1. She <u>is</u> an actress.
2. I <u>am calling</u> to say hello.
3. My brother was <u>writing</u> a report all <u>night</u>.
4. Our teachers <u>were at</u> the soccer <u>game</u> last night.
5. The workers <u>are explaining</u> the problem <u>to</u> the <u>boss</u> now.

Unit 7

1. My <u>dog loves</u> to do tricks.
2. <u>He eats</u> an apple for lunch.
3. <u>They didn't see</u> the problem.
4. <u>She gave</u> some money to the charity.
5. <u>Did</u> the <u>man find</u> his briefcase?
6. Mimi <u>doesn't understand</u> my explanation.

Unit 8

1. Antonio <u>must take</u> math next quarter.
2. We can <u>get good</u> fruit at that <u>fruit</u> stand.
3. Next summer, I <u>should</u> look for <u>a</u> new <u>job</u>.
4. You <u>should exercise</u> every <u>day</u> for your <u>health</u>.
5. They <u>left</u> yesterday because they <u>couldn't</u> find a good <u>hotel</u>.

Unit 9

1. Every day, he <u>cooks</u> rice for <u>dinner</u>.
2. Last week, they <u>visited</u> a park and <u>played</u> tennis.
3. Yesterday, I <u>found</u> a great <u>CD</u>, but I <u>didn't buy</u> it.
4. Now, Ann <u>is waiting</u> for her <u>sister</u> to finish her piano <u>lesson</u>.
5. Every <u>day</u>, we <u>buy</u> a newspaper and <u>look for</u> a new apartment.

Unit 11

1. Tom left class. He went home.
2. I dropped the plate, and it broke.
3. It started to rain. My hair got wet.
4. I felt sad, so I called my good friend.
5. My boss starts work at 7 a.m., but I start at 8 a.m.

Unit 12

1. We arrived at the meeting late.
2. On TV, we saw a program about wild animals.
3. He put the money in the suitcase and took it to the bank.
4. I called my friend from my cell phone, and we made a plan to meet soon.

Unit 13

1. We saw a great movie. It was about a dog.
2. It is necessary to arrive at the airport on time.
3. It takes about 20 minutes for me to drive to the mall.
4. Ken has a lot of friends because it is easy for him to meet people.

Unit 14

1. I don't want to go there in winter.
2. The workers all speak English there.
3. The students worked hard on their project.
4. Most people will share their opinions with you.
5. Famous people often write their autobiographies.
6. There was an important story in the newspaper today.

Unit 16

1. The library was closed yesterday, since it was a holiday.
2. They built a new fire station because the old one was too small.
3. Because the invitation arrived late, I didn't know about the party.
4. Since she finished her report after midnight, she slept only six hours.

Unit 17

1. My uncle has never taken a driving test. (pres perf)
2. We see that strange sign almost every day. (pres)
3. The employees haven't begun to work yet. (pres perf)
4. I have already bought stamps at the post office. (pres perf)
5. My family always eats breakfast early in the morning. (pres)

Unit 18

1. Jack hasn't done his chores yet.
2. We lived in a suburb 14 years ago.
3. We have lived in an apartment since 2004.
4. My family has already decided our vacation plans.
5. Ann felt sick, so she took some medicine and slept all day.

Unit 19

1. That cake needs more sugar.
2. You should make this lemonade sweeter.
3. If you need those chairs, please tell my boss.
4. A famous person signed these documents.

Unit 21

1. In summer, we enjoy swimming.
2. Watching the rain is a nice thing to do.
3. Sitting in the sun gave me a headache.
4. My sister stopped painting last year.
5. I love babies, but their crying keeps me awake at night.

Unit 22

1. Sara became sick from eating some fish.
2. After winning the lottery, my uncle retired.
3. The man was arrested for stealing some money.
4. After painting, my favorite hobby is photography.

Unit 23

1. At my college, all the classes start at 9 a.m.
2. Every passenger should wear a seatbelt.
3. Some birds are building nests in my yard.
4. My brother owns one of the boats in this lake.
5. The children received a lot of presents at the party.

Unit 24

1. In summer, it is fun to travel.
2. Inside this box, there are lots of great CDs.
3. In the fall, I watch movies with my family.
4. For his girlfriend's birthday, Jim bought a gold ring.
5. From Maria's letters, we learned she has a new job.

Unit 26

1. We have to watch the road at all times.

2. We are not supposed to talk on a cell phone and drive.

3. Few drivers are able to drink hot coffee and drive at the same time.

4. You're going to have an accident if you don't pay attention while driving.

Unit 27

1. Although the theater was crowded, Jim found a good seat.

2. Although I have a headache, I need to finish this assignment.

3. Although it's supposed to rain, we'll still have the picnic this afternoon.

4. Although the policeman stopped me for speeding, he didn't give me a ticket.

Unit 28

1. People who are lazy may lose their jobs.

2. I like a partner who is always cheerful.

3. The man who is sitting in the back of the bus looks happy.

4. Ken likes to visit his friend who has a new computer game.

5. Some bosses who are usually happy get upset sometimes.

Unit 29

1. My friend waited for an hour.

2. The car with a sign on top is a taxi.

3. The noise under the bed scared me.

4. The people in my town are very honest.

5. Songs about my country make me sad.

Unit 31

1. The men's race starts at noon.
2. I like his idea, but I really prefer hers.
3. October's days are warm, and its nights are cool.
4. After you read Sara's report, please look at mine.
5. Ken likes to hear his father's stories about his childhood.

Unit 32

1. On weekends, I never rent a DVD. I always go to a movie theater.
2. Some people lose weight by exercising, and others lose it by dieting.
3. Drivers shouldn't talk on cell phones while driving. It can cause an accident.
4. People in my country like to eat in restaurants, but they don't take doggy bags home.
5. Airlines sometimes change departure times, so you should call them before your flight.

Glossary of Grammar Terms

Note: Underlined terms are explained elsewhere in this glossary.

Adjective. This is a word that describes a noun.

> his **beautiful** car
>
> her **yellow** dress
>
> this **old** house

Auxiliary Verb. These verbs appear before <u>main verbs</u>. Some people call them helping verbs. There are three in English: *be* (*am, is, are, was, were*), *do* (*do, does, did*), and *have* (*have, has, had*).

> They **are** eating dinner.
>
> They **have** eaten dinner.
>
> They **do** not eat dinner.

Semi-auxiliary verbs. These verbs are similar to an auxiliary verb. They appear before <u>main verbs</u>. They have two or more words. Some common semi-auxiliary verbs are *be able to, be supposed to, be going to, have to*.

> She **is able to** work with us.
>
> We **are supposed to** work together.
>
> I **am going to** work tomorrow.
>
> They **have to** work all day.

Modal verbs. These verbs are also auxiliary verbs. They appear before <u>main verbs</u>. They are sometimes called modal auxiliary verbs. The common ones are: *can, could, will, would, should, may, might, must*.

> I **can** go with you.
>
> **Should** we go now?
>
> They **might** not go with us.

Base Verb Form. This is also called the dictionary form of a verb. When you look for a verb in a dictionary, you look up the base verb form. For example, *go* is the base verb form for *go, goes, went, gone,* and *going. See* is the base verb form for *see, sees, saw, seen,* and *seeing.*

> What is the meaning of "**go**"?
>
> I need to **go** now.
>
> Can you **go** with me?
>
> Let's **go**!

Clause. This is a group of words that includes both a <u>subject</u> and a <u>verb</u>.

> An **independent clause** can be a <u>sentence</u>.
>
> Dana wants a new computer. (independent clause)

A **dependent clause** has a subject and a verb, but it is not a sentence because it depends on an independent clause.

> because his is not working (dependent clause)
>
> Dana wants a new computer because his is not working.
>
> (a sentence with both an independent and dependent clause)

Compound Sentence. This has two <u>independent clauses</u> connected with a <u>conjunction</u>, such as *and, but, so, or.*

> She felt sick, so she stayed in bed.
>
> Tom will come at noon, and Sue will arrive at 12:30.

Conjunction. This can appear between two <u>independent clauses</u>. In this case, it makes a <u>compound sentence</u>. Some conjunctions are *and, but, so,* and *or.*

> My car is old, **but** I like it.

Dependent Clause. See <u>Clause</u>.

Gerund. A gerund looks like a <u>verb</u> because it is a verb-*ing* form, but it acts like a <u>noun</u>.

Running is good exercise.

I passed the class by **studying** hard.

Independent clause. See <u>**Clause**</u>.

Infinitive. This is *to* + <u>base verb form</u>.

to catch, to pay, to speak

Mari likes **to paint** pictures.

Main Verb. This can be the only <u>verb</u> in a <u>sentence</u>, or it can appear after an <u>auxiliary verb</u>.

Ken **went** to work.

Sarah is **watching** TV.

Ken has **taken** a bus to work.

Modal Verb. See <u>**Auxiliary Verb**</u>.

Noun. This is a word that is used to name a person, place, thing, or quality. It can be the <u>subject</u> in front of a <u>verb</u> or the <u>object</u> of a <u>preposition</u>.

Object. A <u>noun</u> that receives the action of a <u>verb</u>.

Participle. This is a <u>verb</u> form that is used in a verb <u>phrase</u> with one or more <u>auxiliaries</u>.

Present Participle. I am **learning** to play cards.

Past Participle. I have never **played** chess.

Phrase. A phrase is two or more words that form a unit.

> my two friends (noun phrase)
>
> have been practicing (verb phrase)
>
> for several hours (prepositional phrase)
>
> My two friends have been practicing for several hours. (independent clause/or sentence with three phrases)

Preposition. This appears before a <u>noun</u>. Generally, it shows a place, time, or direction. Some prepositions are *in, to, for, of, at, on, near, by, from*.

> We went **to** the store.
>
> He left **at** midnight.

Prepositional phrase. This is a group of words that includes a <u>preposition</u> and a <u>noun</u>.

> He put his money **in his pocket.** (*In his pocket* is a prepositional phrase. The word *in* is the preposition and *pocket* is the noun.)
>
> **At night,** we sometimes watch a movie. (The expression *at night* is a prepositional phrase. The word *at* is the preposition and *night* is the noun.)

Semi-Auxiliary Verb. See **<u>Auxiliary Verb</u>**.

Sentence. This is an independent grammatical unit that has at least one <u>subject</u> and one <u>verb</u>. It begins with a capital letter and ends with a period (.), question mark (?), or exclamation point (!).

Subject. This can be a <u>noun</u>, noun phrase, or pronoun in a <u>sentence</u> or <u>clause</u>. It identifies the "doer" of the action.

Verb. A verb expresses an action that is done by the <u>subject</u>.

Common Irregular Verbs

BASE FORM	PAST	PAST PARTICIPLE	PRESENT PARTICIPLE
begin	began	begun	beginning
break	broke	broken	breaking
bring	brought	brought	bringing
buy	bought	bought	buying
catch	caught	caught	catching
choose	chose	chosen	choosing
come	came	come	coming
cost	cost	cost	costing
do	did	done	doing
drink	drank	drunk	drinking
drive	drove	driven	driving
eat	ate	eaten	eating
fall	fell	fallen	falling
feel	felt	felt	feeling
find	found	found	finding
forget	forgot	forgotten	forgetting
get	got	gotten	getting
give	gave	given	giving
go	went	gone	going
have	had	had	having
hear	heard	heard	hearing
hurt	hurt	hurt	hurting
know	knew	known	knowing
leave	left	left	leaving

BASE FORM	PAST	PAST PARTICIPLE	PRESENT PARTICIPLE
lose	lost	lost	losing
make	made	made	making
mean	meant	meant	meaning
meet	met	met	meeting
quit	quit	quit	quitting
read	read	read	reading
ride	rode	ridden	riding
ring	rang	rung	ringing
run	ran	run	running
say	said	said	saying
see	saw	seen	seeing
send	sent	sent	sending
sing	sang	sung	singing
sit	sat	sat	sitting
sleep	slept	slept	sleeping
speak	spoke	spoken	speaking
stand	stood	stood	standing
take	took	taken	taking
teach	taught	taught	teaching
tell	told	told	telling
think	thought	thought	thinking
throw	threw	thrown	throwing
wake	woke	woken	waking
win	won	won	winning
write	wrote	written	writing

Other Books of Interest
from Pro Lingua Associates
Also by David Kehe and Peggy Dustin Kehe

Write after Input. A text teaching students to develop paragraphs and compositions based on listening and reading input. The students progress through five units from constructing a single, basic paragraph to writing a five-paragraph composition.

Writing Strategies. Two texts jam-packed with writing activities. Each covers four modes of writing. Book One (intermediate) teaches description, narration, exposition, and comparison and contrast. Book Two (advanced) covers process, cause and effect, extended definition, and argumentation. Coordinated with these lessons are fluency writing exercises and lessons on grammar problems and terminology.

Conversation Strategies. 29 structured pair activities for developing strategic conversation skills at the intermediate level. Students learn the words, phrases, and conventions used by native speakers in the active give-and-take of everyday conversation.

Discussion Strategies. Carefully structured pair and small-group work at the advanced-intermediate level. Excellent preparation for students who will participate in academic or professional work that requires effective participation in discussion and seminars.

OTHER BOOKS ON GRAMMAR

The Modal Book. Fourteen units explore the form, meaning, and use of the American English modal verb system, one semantic group at a time. Each unit also explores the sights and sounds of a different country, from Brazil to Turkey.

Shenanigames. A photocopyable collection of 49 games and activities that bring a wide range of grammar points to life.

A Phrasal Verb Affair. When John runs out on Maria and runs off with another woman, Maria tracks him down to do him in. Fifteen dramatic episodes in the style of a soap opera introduce the learners to over 200 phrasal verbs. Lots of exercises. The text is accompanied by a dramatization of the script on a CD.

QUESTIONS? SIMPLY GIVE US A CALL
AND WE'LL TRY TO HELP!
802-257-7779